# Children are People
## The Librarian in the Community

*Hamish Hamilton Books for*
*the Professional Librarian*

ANNE CARROLL MOORE
A Biography
By Frances Clarke Sayers

BOOKS IN SEARCH OF CHILDREN
Speeches and Essays
by Louise Seaman Bechtel
Edited and Introduced by
Virginia Haviland

# Children are People

The Librarian in the Community

## Janet Hill

Hamish Hamilton

First published in Great Britain 1973 by
Hamish Hamilton Children's Books Ltd.
90 Great Russell Street, London WC1B 3PT

ISBN 0 241 02243 6

Printed in Great Britain by
Western Printing Services Ltd, Bristol

To M. C. L.

# Contents

# Illustrations

# Author's Note

My thanks are due to so many people who have helped to make this book possible. It is based on my experience in Lambeth, which is a stimulating and exciting library system in which to work and where staff are given responsibility and encouraged to think. Work with children in Lambeth exists within the framework of a total philosophy of librarianship which has been built up over the years and undoubtedly owes most to the inspiration and ideas of our Director, Roy McColvin. The debt I owe to him is incalculable.

In recent years I have also been grateful for the support, help and wonderfully practical advice of Ted Rubidge, our Assistant Director; and for the frequent opportunities for discussion with my colleagues involved in other aspects of the library service. This now includes the staff responsible for the Recreation Service, who have contributed a breadth of outlook, imagination, and a freshness of approach which makes the future development of the service to children, working in close liaison with them, seem a most exciting challenge to face.

A library service must be based on teamwork. I never cease to be grateful to the innumerable lively, talented, dedicated and enthusiastic staff who have worked with children in Lambeth in the past and also those who do so today. They are the key people by whom a library service must be judged because they are the ones in daily contact with the public.

For several years I have been fortunate to have Jenny Evans working with me as The Assistant Children's Librarian and it is no accident that there has been a swift acceleration in the development of the service to children since she joined the staff. She gives more time and energy to her job than anyone has the right to expect.

Without the people I have mentioned there would have been no book to write. Without the good humour, patience and encouragement of my editor, Julia MacRae, it would certainly never have been written, and I am most grateful for her support.

My thanks are also due to Mike Hailstone, who took most of the photographs; and to Pam Lane who typed the manuscript for me with such painstaking care and efficiency.

J.H.

# I
# Children and the Children's Librarian

What a crazy place—this must be the second home of every budding comedian and circus artist for miles . . . a great session, some real participation, and the repartee was fun. A good time was had by all—especially those trying without success to edge the storyteller backwards into the water. . . .

Report on a storytelling session held by Lambeth librarians in a very temporary adventure playground. 1971.

Librarians working with children need, even more than other librarians, a sense of vocation. The work is not easy, because sometimes children, particularly if there are many of them milling round in the library at the same time, can cause commotion, and disrupt the peaceful usage of the library.

*Library work with children* by Roy Harrod. 1969.

The two quotations express rather different views on the role of the librarian. There is little doubt about which is the more familiar one. According to the traditional stereotype, children's librarians tend to be pleasant, gentle, mild-mannered, good tempered, unwilling to offend, extremely hard-working, dedicated to their profession, and almost totally unaware of the world outside children's books and libraries. There is a strong element of truth in this description. The early pioneers of children's librarianship both in this country and the United States were made of sterner stuff. If they had not been, they would never have been able to establish the importance of libraries for children, and earned the gratitude of those who follow in their footsteps. It is interesting to read Eileen Colwell's modest account of the beginnings of her career in an unnamed Lancashire cotton town, and her move to Hendon in the late 1920's to build up a children's library service, starting literally from nothing. Without her determination, strength of character and strong convictions, it is difficult to see how she could have achieved anything at all. In the United States, where children's librarianship developed earlier than in England, Frances Clarke Sayers's recent biography shows that Anne Carroll Moore of New York Public Library was a dynamic and formidable as well as an eccentric woman. The fact that her influence is still active in the New York library system is apparent to anyone who has worked there as I have. These and many other librarians throughout the history of the profession have defied the stereotype.

However, there are still too many librarians today who fit the description only too accurately. They could be forgiven for thinking they are just what the profession needs. Certainly this is the impression they would get from descriptions of ideal children's librarians in library textbooks and in children's literature, and even sometimes in career guides. There has always been a tendency for writers to pontificate about the character of the ideal children's librarian. W. C. Berwick Sayers in his *Manual of Children's Libraries* published in 1926 wrote: 'So we may assume that a children's librarian must be a person of good education, solid nerves, and attractive to youngsters. . . .'

Even earlier, in a paper given at a Conference on Public Education and the Public Libraries, Children's Section, 1903, John Ballinger, writing on the idea of setting up children's reading halls said: 'The greatest factor in its success will be the superintendent. For this post a sympathetic, well-educated woman, with organizing ability and of good temper, should be selected if possible.'

I rather like the 'if possible'!

In *Libraries for Children* published in 1961, Lionel McColvin wrote:

The successful children's librarian has certain essential personal gifts, the first of which is common sense, which means that she must be able to take things as they are, to do simply what the situation requires, without fuss, to give and take, to be tolerant, to be practical. Then she must be placid and patient.

As late as 1969, Roy Harrod gave his version in *Library Work with Children*:

What sort of person makes a good children's librarian? Primarily and fundamentally one who is friendly, a good mixer, of sound character and having much commonsense; she must be patient, not easily put out by misbehaviour or pressure of work, remaining calm at all times; she must like children and be tolerant of them and their ways and also of her colleagues; she must be willing to turn her hand to any job that needs to be done in the department even if it is normally done by people junior to herself.

What a boring composite character these descriptions conjure up! One can just see legions of children's librarians, placidly smiling as they cope uncomplainingly and self-effacingly with obstreperous children and difficult chief librarians, invariably making common-sense decisions as they go about their routine tasks. This image is surely not super-human but sub-human. I think it is insulting to suggest that a librarian who works with children should comply with rigid character specifications. It is insulting to children as well as to librarians. Children are neither two-headed monsters nor wide-eyed innocents. They are people.

The children's librarian in children's literature is usually portrayed sympathetically, and again a fairly clear composite picture emerges, and one which is obviously intended by authors to be flattering. It seems to be without question that the children's librarian is female, generally helpful, friendly and approachable but hardly dynamic. In several cases, before the end of the novel, she becomes sedately engaged to a nice young man, and is undoubtedly set to fade out into a peaceful marriage. Although there was the case of the long-defunct Molly Hilton, heroine of one of the early career novels, who was distinguished by the fact that unlike the heroines of all other books in the series, she failed to get her man by the end of the last chapter. As the career novels were read as light romances, this was a singular failure on the part of the author, who I believe was subsequently persuaded by pressure from librarians to take the unprecedented step of writing a sequel in which Molly finally became engaged to a librarian, although she primly refused to take even this step before she was elected to the Library Association register as a fully qualified librarian! Miss Turner in Jean George's *My Side of the Mountain* is a dependable ally, and encourages Sam to find the site of his great-grandfather's farm in the Catskill mountains. When Sam explains that he plans to go and settle on the site, living off nuts and berries and by trapping animals, her reaction is both sedate and sensible. 'Miss Turner was the only person that believed me. She smiled, sat back in her chair and said "Well, I declare".'

After he has become firmly established in the Catskills, he pays a return visit to the library, and Miss Turner points out that he needs a haircut:

> She thought a minute, got out her library scissors, and sat me down on the back steps. She did a fine job, and I looked like any other boy who had played hard all day, and who, with a little soap and water after supper, would be going off to bed in a regular house.

In Sydney Taylor's *All of a Kind Family*, set in New York in 1912, on New York's Lower East Side, the family meets the 'library lady' in Chapter I, when Sarah has to report with much trepidation that she has lost her library book. Miss Allen is kind but firm, and Sarah agrees to pay a penny a week towards the cost. Library visits and encounters with Miss Allen feature as a regular part of their life, and eventually when she is invited to celebrate a Jewish festival with them, it turns out that their other guest, Charlie, a long-time friend of the family is Miss Allen's long-lost love.

Rufus M in the book of that name, is so-called because he cannot write the rest of his surname 'Moffat' on the library card, when with much tenacity he survives the pleasant but firm approach of the librarian who not only sends him to wash his hands, but shows him how to print his name. When he gets back triumphant with his mother's signature on the by now scruffy card only to find the library closed, he ingeniously climbs in through the cellar, and surprises the librarian having tea in a back room. Rufus sticks his ground, and eventually the librarian lets him take a book home. It is an amusing incident, but I do find the librarian a bit too good to be true.

It is interesting that *My Side of the Mountain*, *All of a Kind Family*, and *Rufus M* are all American books, first published in 1959, 1951 and 1943 respectively. The only English book I can recall in which a children's librarian features to such an extent is Dorothy Clewes's short story *Library Lady* in which the plot involves a theft from a library exhibition. The six-year-old heroine Ginny, is a regular visitor to the small neighbourhood library in the High Street. She gets to know the librarian, who within the limits of a story of only fifty-six pages, is depicted as unobtrusively helpful and friendly.

Not surprisingly, the Last Apple Gang in E. W. Hildick's *Jim Starling and the Colonel* don't have a confrontation with a children's librarian, but with a 'tall, brawny young woman' in the Reference Library. She greets them with reluctance, and expels them with speed when Terry, flushed with triumph at making an important discovery so far forgets himself as to shout 'dopes' in a loud voice, shattering the studious silence.

But let Philippa Pearce have the last word, in her perfect and all too credible cameo of an adult librarian whose sense of ordered priority is disturbed by a child actually borrowing a book from the adult library in *A Dog so Small*: Ben has exhausted the dog books in the children's library, and after several conversations while he tries to find out more about Chihuahuas, decides to take out a book called *Dogs of the World*.

> The librarian, watching him go out with the book under his arm, still felt uneasy. She was sure there was something wrong somewhere, even if she could not put her finger upon it. She would feel happier, anyway, when he went back to the Junior Library, where he belonged.

Another view of children's librarians is given in *Careers for Girls* by Ruth Miller. The description reads:

> Almost invariably a woman. She is responsible for the choice and arrangement of her stock. She also organises a wide range of 'extension activities,' such as story afternoons, puppet clubs, scrapbooks for exchange with children's libraries abroad, discussion and review afternoons (when the children review books for their own and younger age groups) and all sorts of activities which may help children to appreciate books and reading.
>
> She will also liase with local schools. She may help to stock school libraries, she may co-operate with teachers on special 'projects' and, in school hours, she may be asked to teach children how to make the best use of libraries generally, and reference books in particular.

What an inspiring picture! Could anything be more calculated to encourage lively and imaginative school leavers of both sexes with at least two A-levels and three O-levels to take up librarianship? This book was first published in 1966, but was 'fully revised' in 1970!

To be fair, there are probably still librarians who would consider that an adequate description of the scope of their work, although there is nothing in it which could not have been written in the 1920's.

What situation does the modern urban librarian who works with children face in the 70's? It is a banal observation that we live in a period of unprecedented flux and change. Some barriers break down, while others, supremely the class divisions in our society, deepen and intensify. Ideas, standards and organizations once accepted without question, are under attack. Children are processed through the educational machine, and too many of them emerge scarred for life, without any experience of real education at all. Platitudes are mouthed about the importance of the first five years of life, and only patchwork and inadequate measures are taken to ensure that even some children are given proper opportunities to develop at this stage. The inner areas of our large cities are developing the familiar problems of overcrowding, slum housing, dire poverty, racial tensions, loneliness and misery. All of these generalizations affect children who are growing up in the British Isles today. In our own particular field, how much is said and written about 'reading problems'. Backward readers, reluctant learners, emotionally deprived, culturally disadvantaged—the fashionable terms change with rapidity, as do the programmes from Educational Priority Areas to Urban Aid. What is certain is that the problems are immense, and they do not lessen. For many, many years people have reiterated the dilemmas. As Ivan Illich wrote recently in *Deschooling Society*:

> It should be obvious that even with schools of equal quality a poor child can seldom catch up with a rich one. Even if they attend equal schools and begin at the same age, poor children lack most of the educational opportunities which are casually available to the middle-class child. These advantages range from conversations and books in the home to vacation travel and a different sense of oneself, and apply, for the child who enjoys them, both in and out of school.

All this is hardly news to anyone who works with children in a mixed community. The publication in 1972 of *From Birth to Seven*, a study produced by the National Children's Bureau of nearly 16,000 seven-year-old children who were all born during one week in

March 1958, gave positive and detailed proof of the disadvantages suffered by working class children, and in particular by those from semi-skilled and unskilled families. The study covers the health, home background, behaviour, physical attributes, abilities and achievements of the children, who had also been the subject of a perinatal mortality study at birth. It analyses housing conditions and relates them to reading attainment:

> The results for reading attainment indicate that both overcrowding and basic amenities are important. The effect of overcrowding is equivalent to two or three months retardation in reading age in the context of this analysis. The effect of absence—or shared use—of all basic amenities is equivalent to about nine months retardation in reading age.

Nearly half of the children from unskilled families were poor readers at the age of seven, compared with only one in twelve from professional families. More than one in twenty of children from unskilled families were judged to need special schooling, whilst fewer than one in five hundred children from professional families needed special schooling. Children from unskilled families were on average shorter, had poorer oral ability and poorer general knowledge as well as being more likely to have various physical defects.

Sir Alec Clegg, the well-known Chief Education Officer of the West Riding of Yorkshire, giving the 1972 Convocation Lecture to the National Children's Home said:

> The bitter fact about the majority of children who are atypical because of some form of deprivation is that it is those whose lives stand most in need of enrichment who are often the last to get it. . . .
> They lack books and a quiet place to read and such a place must be provided for them. They need space that the home all too often cannot provide and they need materials with which to experiment. They need to get to know the places of interest within their environment and they can often best be stimulated to educational endeavour by being taken to places of interest beyond it. They need to see beauty in its many forms in nature and in art, and above all, they themselves need to learn to use, and to enjoy using, their own creative powers.

The inadequacy of provision for pre-school children in this country is shown up almost every week in articles, books, letters to the press and discussion on nursery schools and pre-school play-groups. Again to quote *From Birth to Seven*:

> Over and above this, environmental influences will shape a child's abilities and influence his capacity or readiness to learn. A great deal—if not the major part—of learning takes place outside of school and much of this is accomplished even before the child enters school. The vocabulary and concepts used by those around him are vital in providing a framework within which his own intellectual growth can take place. If this framework is bare or impoverished, his own development is likely to be slow; a rich framework of words and ideas will provide the food for more rapid growth.

In many parts of the country, and certainly in most of our largest cities, there are children who share the disadvantages already mentioned, but are also disadvantaged because they are black. Anyone who still doubts this (and incredibly there are people who do) should read what black people say about the situation. Bernard Coard in his depressing book *How the West Indian Child is made Educationally Subnormal in the British School System* writes about his experience as a teacher in an ESN School. In a mixed class of black and white children, all the paintings and drawings of themselves and each other by the class were *white*. Bernard Coard experimented by drawing himself a picture of a West Indian boy in the class. He drew the outline, then began to shade the face black. The boy who was his model said:

> What—what are you doing? You are *spoiling* me!
> I said: No, of course not. I am painting you as you are—Black; just like I am. Black *is* beautiful, you know. You aren't ashamed of that, are you?
> At that he calmed down, and I completed shading his face black. Then I did his hair. His hair was black, short, and very African in texture. I drew it exactly as his hair really was. When he saw it, he jumped out of his chair and shouted: 'You painted me to look like a golliwog! You make me look just like a golliwog!'

The author points out the ways in which the confidence of the black child is undermined, and included are the following reasons:

> . . . by totally ignoring the Black child's language, history, culture, identity. Through the choice of teaching materials, the society emphasizes who and what it thinks is important—and by implication, by omission, who and what it thinks

is unimportant, infinitesimal, irrelevant. Through the belittling, ignoring or denial of a person's identity, one can destroy perhaps the most important aspect of a person's personality—his sense of identity, of who he is. Without this he will get nowhere.

The opportunities for development and growth children are given reflect unmistakably the values of the society to which they belong. There should be no excuse for anyone who works in local government to be politically naïve. Can any children's librarian claim the right to be politically unaware? Can anyone who works with children fail to be interested in legislation which affects children, and in the conditions under which children are growing up?

An effective librarian needs to be both realistic and idealistic about what it is possible to achieve within the context of contemporary society. Is our stereotyped children's librarian equipped to cope? Of course not. I believe that many librarians in the past, and unfortunately many still coming into the profession, have had little preparation for the frustrations as well as the challenge of trying to practise librarianship today. I have personally seen more frustration and disillusionment amongst staff who have plunged enthusiastically into running a children's library in a difficult area than I care to remember. I am certainly very conscious of my own failure to help staff in this situation in the past. I have known staff leave, whether they admitted it or not, because they could no longer take the daily disappointment of trying to find books for children who could barely read at the age of ten, or because having made real contact with some of the children, they were unable to cope with the intensive testing to which they were then subjected by those same children, who could not believe that they had found an adult prepared to show some interest in them. There must be many children's libraries which are used mainly by children who are poor readers, or by children who see the library only as a temporary refuge during the holidays and evenings, rather than as a place to read or borrow books. Such libraries can be depressing if you understand why this situation exists, and develop a philosophy which leads you not just to accept the fact, but to relate it to the total situation of society, and understand the limits of what you as a single individual can do about it.

It is not I think, unfair to claim that there has been, and still is, a tendency to expect children's librarians to be a little short on intellect. This attitude is not confined to Britain, as is shown in an essay *Of Memory and Muchness* by the American, Frances Clarke Sayers, in her *Summoned by Books*:

> As for children's librarians themselves, they are often attractive, young and pleasant. But as far as intellect and the serious business of librarianship, there is sometimes a lifting of the eyebrow on the part of the serious among us, and a shrugging dismissal of the clan as a whole. I have read too many dossiers in library schools not to know whereof I speak. 'Not strong in background or scholarship. She might make a good children's librarian.'

Recently I came across a student taking the degree course in librarianship in one of the better-known Colleges of Librarianship. She had quite a struggle to persuade them that she was serious in wanting to get some of her practical experience on the course in working with children. She was told during her discussions about this that if she wanted to work with children, she should not be taking the degree course!

A librarian is concerned, amongst other things, with selecting, assessing and rejecting books. This requires a degree of intellect, apart from any other aspect of the work. Anyone who begins work within the confines of a library, with the modest ambition of getting to know the converted (that is, the children who for a variety of reasons do regularly visit the library) and providing a carefully chosen bookstock for them will soon run into difficulties. The natural reading tastes of children are generally far removed from those of most reviewers of children's books. There is a vast difference between the glib, euphoric talk that is heard of the 'new golden age of children's books' and the reality of the librarian faced with the infinite variety of children and the limitations of the bookstock. One of the hardest facts with which a librarian has to come to terms, is that however generous the book fund, however enlightened the book selection policy, it is only possible to select a stock from the books *which have been published*. Librarians should be vocal in their attacks on books which are not good enough for children. They should also be capable of critical well-informed and sophisticated criticism of the books which *are* good. Again, is our stereotyped children's librarian equipped to cope? Of course not.

Naturally there are innumerable individual exceptions to generalizations about stereotyped librarians. But is there much *evidence* to prove my generalization wrong? Do most children's librarians see their work in the context of society today? Do most think the problems children face in getting books, reading books, and finding books to which they can relate, are problems they should be thinking about? Do many publicly discuss and write about such issues? Do many have a reputation for reviewing books? Do many write to the national press when issues affecting children's books arise? Do many discuss what form children's librarianship could take in twenty or even ten years time? I certainly hope many do. But the evidence is sparse.

# 2
# The Contemporary Context of Librarianship

Children's librarians have tended to become isolated. Their national organization, the Youth Libraries Group (YLG) of the Library Association, certainly has. One of the reasons for this is the way it is organized. Local branches operate in different areas throughout the country, and serve some purpose in providing the opportunity for librarians to meet together, attend talks by speakers or one-day courses. This is undoubtedly useful, if hardly dynamic, but is not likely to encourage any real developments in thinking about work with children. Probably it has most value in places where librarians are geographically isolated.

The branches are represented on the national committee, to which members are also elected annually. This national committee meets at the most four times a year, usually in London, for one day at a time. As travelling expenses of committee members are paid by YLG, the reason given for limiting the meetings to four annually is that it would be too expensive to meet more often. Surely it should be possible to overcome the financial problems in the interests of greater efficiency? If the committee met more often, at least it would be able to react with more alacrity to matters which need immediate attention. I would not deny that many people work extremely hard and devotedly on the committee, and believe it has some value. To call a committee *well-meaning* is a deadly accolade, but unfortunately it is the most accurate description of YLG. Certainly I found my own brief period on the committee a deeply depressing experience, and in common with many other librarians I know, decided it was a complete waste of time to have anything to do with it. I found the committee distinctly unprofessional. The minutes were bland in the extreme, whatever the discussions may have been; professional criticism was invariably construed as personal attack; and there was an unwillingness ever to challenge the parent body, the Library

Association. Although this was certainly not true of individual members of the committee, its corporate image was, and still is, that of the stereotype children's librarian, pleasant, mild, and lacking in impact. There is a need for young enthusiastic librarians to get themselves elected to the committee in such large numbers that they can bring about radical alterations both in the work the committee does, and in the way it operates.

One of the saddest things about YLG is that it never seems to get involved in issues which arise in the outside world and concern children's librarianship. It would, no doubt, have been gratifying to *The Guardian* if their initiative in establishing an annual children's fiction award in 1967 had been publicly recognized by a letter from YLG congratulating them; it would have been fitting if YLG had contributed a well-reasoned letter to the lengthy correspondence in *The Times* on *Little Black Sambo* in 1972. A response to such matters may seem a small thing, but at least it might help to convince people that YLG was *there*.

YLG hold an annual weekend school. It has followed the same inevitable pattern as long as I can remember, and I can remember a long time. The 1972 model was called *Working Together*. The sub-title read: 'The conference aims to bring together all interested in promoting children's books—teachers, parents, lecturers, book-sellers, reviewers and librarians'. I have been to that conference many times over in my professional life. There is an opportunity to meet and chat with professional colleagues, a series of talks followed by questions, and usually one discussion period. It could be argued that new entrants to the profession have not been through all this before, and might find it valuable and conceivably enjoyable. Wouldn't it be more valuable to make the basis of the weekend seminars and discussions about real issues, where there might be some give and take between young librarians and those who have been around for some time? I am sure many librarians felt as I did on seeing the programme for 1972—that they had neither the time nor the inclination to go all the way to Stirling for a pleasant weekend in September, complete with afternoon tea at Scone Palace. YLG conspicuously lacks a sense of *urgency*. There are children out there wanting books and not getting them, many unable to read if they can get them; large-scale local government re-organization is almost upon us; spending on books for schools is scandalously low in many parts of the country—topics it would be both fruitful and possibly constructive to discuss are endless. Other professional conferences make statements, pass resolutions, urge action. When will YLG weekend schools hit the headlines in the national press? Devoted committee members work extremely hard to make them the success I am sure they are in their own terms. But it is all such a waste.

YLG is responsible for the annual Carnegie and Kate Greenaway book awards, the former given to an outstanding book published the previous year, the latter for illustration. A book could be written about the unfortunate gaucheries surrounding this annual event. I shall refer to the actual choice of books in a later chapter, but publishers, writers, artists and reviewers can produce a fund of stories about the mishandling of the award ceremony over the years. Many of these can be attributed to officials of the Library Association rather than members of the YLG committee, but it should be possible to make vociferous protests about such mismanagement in the right quarters. Usually the celebration of the award takes the form of a dinner. Most organizations planning such an event with small funds would probably settle for a short reception with drinks and snacks rather than a full meal. These may seem trivial points, but the whole purpose of a function to celebrate an award is surely to honour the recipient, and make the occasion a memorable one for everyone who attends. It is salutary and shaming to read Lucy Boston's description in *Memory in a House* of her experiences as a recipient of the Carnegie Medal. How sad that this is the only published account of a writer's reaction to what should have been, and clearly was not, an enjoyable occasion. A lack of sophistication and imagination, often a lack of basic good manners, seem to characterize this and other YLG events. To be fair, YLG are not alone in this. Librarians generally have a very bad reputation as far as entertaining and looking after guests is concerned. Most publishers and writers can produce depressing stories of how they were treated when invited to speak at conferences, or at an individual library. People have been invited to speak without being offered a fee, or offered one so paltry that it is insulting; travelling expenses claimed have been queried; speakers invited to take part in an all-day conference have been left to fend for themselves at lunch—the examples are legion. Most of it surely can only stem from unawareness, as I cannot believe it is intended to deliberately insult speakers, or to make people feel uncomfortable.

Too many children's librarians have become isolated from the rest of their profession. There are historical reasons for this. The early pioneers fought hard to establish that work with children should be recognized as a specialist branch of librarianship. Children's libraries were set up, and the need for those working with children to undergo some specific form of training became apparent. These developments were essential and we have every reason to be grateful to those early librarians who had the foresight and determination to struggle for what they believed in. What they did was necessary, but it has led us into an impossible situation today. There are librarians who have come to believe not only that children's librarians are different but also that children are different. Even worse, many children's librarians seem to believe this too.

Children's librarians have made so much fuss about the importance of specially trained staff working with children that many librarians seem to have decided that if they are working with adults in a public library situation, they should not be expected to have anything to do with children. Equally, because of the value placed on the study of children's literature, many librarians who have not studied this field consider themselves completely exonerated from the responsibility for knowing anything about children's books at all. The corollary of this is that there are even children's librarians who read *only* children's books.

Just as the movement to establish the value of trained children's librarians has led many people into a situation of total and self-imposed withdrawal from the rest of the profession, so the pressures to develop adequate library services for children have led many people into persuading themselves that everything about children's librarianship, even, for example, the method of ordering books, should be different. So children's librarians have laid a snare for

*Above:* Children listening to a Jamaican folk music session

*Below:* Listening to a story

Showing picture book films at a One O'Clock Club

themselves, in which many of them seem to be inescapably trapped. In how many authorities has the children's librarian so jealously guarded the 'difference' of the children's library that qualified children's librarians are even engaged in such clerical activities as writing overdue notices for books, when a clerical or junior assistant should deal with such items for the whole library service? It sounds ludicrous, but it happens. I believe that many if not most children's librarians are extremely hard-working and conscientious. This applies both to those in supervisory posts, who should be referred to as supervising children's librarians, and those in day to day contact with children who are practising librarians. If there are practising librarians who spend a large proportion of their time in what might be described as the housekeeping duties in a children's library, tidying the shelves and engaging in such activities as actually withdrawing books from stock (as opposed to making decisions about which books should be withdrawn from stock), there are certainly supervising librarians who spend a proportion of their time on activities like classifying and cataloguing children's books. Now a case can be made for a simplified system of classification for children's books, but what kind of logic is it for this to be done by a specialist in children's books? Surely it should be done by the staff who specialize in cataloguing and classification? Recently at one of the six-monthly informal meetings of the London 'senior children's librarians' (a blanket term devised to describe the supervising children's librarians in the 32 London boroughs) we were asked by one member of the group to fill in a questionnaire. The purpose was to find out how we ordered books, whether we wrote out order slips, or did we by any chance order books through the same channels as the adult library? This is a not unfair example of the level of discussion at these meetings, and it indicates a very depressing state of affairs. It is all part of the 'children's librarian must deal with everything in the children's library' syndrome carried to a supervisory level.

If children's librarians want to be freed from all these extraneous routines so that they have time to consider their work in relation to children of the 70's, the first thing they must do is begin to think differently about themselves. The point has always been made that children's librarianship can be a quiet backwater, and that once anyone has specialized, chances of promotion outside children's librarianship are extremely limited, and of course this is very true. There must be many librarians initially fired with enthusiasm who decided regretfully that children's librarianship was a blind alley: another insulting aspect of the tendency to assume that children's librarians were pleasant and mild-mannered was that they were female and would either marry and therefore it did not matter as their careers would be at an end, or they were sufficiently dedicated to spend their working lives uncomplaining and underpaid, because they enjoyed working with children. Clearly in modern terms these views are laughable. It is surely time we stopped expecting librarians to specialize so rigidly for all time in one aspect of librarianship? Should we any more have librarians who only work with children? If children's librarians should come back into the mainstream of librarianship, and if we expect all librarians to accept children as people, and to participate in providing a library service for them, shouldn't children's librarians accept adults as people too, and possibly even work with them? The divisions have become completely artificial. If librarians have the opportunity of working with children from time to time, many of them would be able to contribute a great deal. Equally, children's librarians, who at least have a better record for actually reading books, could influence their colleagues working with adults. Sometimes children's librarians are quite fatalistic about the fact there are still comparatively few men working with children in libraries. Given a greater flexibility there would undoubtedly be far more. The trouble is that some children's librarians have got so carried away by the 'specialist' nature of their work that they have built up a great mystique around it. Some of them have even come to believe that only children's librarians can tell stories or give talks to children adequately. Happily, there are many places where such ideas are being proved nonsensical, but they are still very much in the minority. And why once a children's librarian always a children's librarian?

So many of the problems spring from nothing more than the fact that the children's library and children, and also the children's librarian, are treated as different. False situations are created, non-existent problems are raised. Would a visitor from another planet credit that some eighty years after children's libraries began to develop, librarians can still be heard discussing what age a child should be allowed to join the library or when a child should be allowed to borrow books from the adult library? Or that there is still in some quarters a tendency to regard the children's library as a rather homespun little place which has no connection with the professionally run adult library? I particularly like the hoary old suggestion in some of the dated textbooks on librarianship that children will feel more at home if they are allowed to assist in routine duties as 'junior helpers'. Could anything be more ridiculous? It has always been one of my ambitions to write an article suggesting that old age pensioners would feel more at home in the adult library if they did volunteer shifts filing catalogue cards.

If children's librarians want this kind of situation to alter, they have a chance of bringing changes if they can be persuaded to think differently. Otherwise they are trapped in a vicious circle. For this reason, the reaction of children's librarians generally to changes in the library service in the London Borough of Camden in 1969 was extremely depressing. An article by Frank Cole, Deputy Director of Libraries and Arts for Camden in *Youth Libraries Group News*, (June 1970) spelt out the new approach they have adopted. In July 1969 the London Borough's Management Services Unit recommended 'that the post of Head of Children's Services be disestablished at an appropriate time and that the service be placed under the control of the Head of Lending Services'. As this recommendation coincided almost exactly with the retirement of the previous holder of this position, the report was adopted forthwith. Thirteen librarians are responsible for the library service to children in the fourteen Camden libraries. One is designated as Senior Children's Librarian, and based at the busiest library. The four next in seniority are designated as children's librarians, and also as second in charge of the branch at their respective libraries. This dual role aims to give librarians wider experience than they would gain working only with children. As Frank Cole wrote: 'The value of narrow specialization has often been questioned.' There is no doubt at all that Camden provides a good library service for children.

Frank Cole himself has long been an enthusiastic member of the London and Home Counties Branch of the Youth Libraries Group. Camden had become concerned about the tendency to separate off children's work from the rest of librarianship, and this is the method they have chosen to try to counteract this narrowness of approach. They are in no sense denigrating the value of library work with children, nor has it hindered growth of the service as two more children's librarians have been appointed since the system was changed. Interestingly, the Camden children's librarians, many of whom have years of experience, seem happy about the situation themselves. But at the time this scheme was inaugurated there was an outcry amongst children's librarians generally. The reaction was obviously subjective. Children's librarians clearly were saying to themselves 'Could this ever happen to me?' There were dark hints that this marked the beginning of the holocaust. It is very sad that children's librarians should have reacted so defensively to what is essentially an experimental and different way of running a library service. I don't imagine Camden saw themselves as setting a trend that other people would follow. That might happen, equally it might not. There should be nothing sacrosanct about the pattern of a library service, and there is room for many different approaches. Growth cannot happen without experiment. Certainly Camden's philosophy is different from ours in Lambeth, for example, but surely no one would be so arrogant as to claim that there could only be one approach to running a library service? Camden felt that children's librarianship had become inbred and isolated, and they have found a different way of tackling this problem from the one we have chosen.

If children's librarians are going to react hysterically every time a library system with a good record of services to children adopts a different line, even if this does involve abolishing a senior post in children's work, then it is a very sad reflection on our profession. If children's librarianship is to be closely integrated into the rest of the profession, where does that get us? Let no outsider have any doubts that librarianship is a rather curious business. Take books, which should be a good starting point. Too many librarians are not very interested in books, and don't read much. Ask them what their views are about the future or the purpose of libraries, and you will get a very confused answer. What will be clear, is that beyond making the assumption that because there have been public libraries for over a hundred years, there always will be libraries, and that they are vaguely educational and/or cultural and/or recreational establishments, they don't see the need to give the matter any further thought. There have been too few leaders of real vision in the higher echelons of librarianship, and the evidence is seen in libraries which complacently muddle along without any clear sense of purpose, and obviously without having seen the need to work out a philosophy, even to justify their own existence. There were, and still are, librarians who made their names by pursuing different forms of gadgetry. There were those who made the tools of librarianship, like cataloguing, their speciality. There were librarians who talked knowledgeably and enthusiastically about every aspect of library buildings. Every generation has fresh opportunities for becoming sidetracked. Currently many are dazzled by computers, though probably more by audio-visual aids and resource centres. No one aware of contemporary developments in the arts and in teaching methods would deny that audio-visual aids must have a place in libraries. Resource centres are a sensible idea. The term can be simply defined as a library in which all book and non-book materials are assembled together in a unified collection which is administered as a whole. However, to hear some librarians talk of audio-visual aids and resource centres with bated breath as though they will solve all our problems, can only induce an attitude of cynicism amongst those librarians who are aware that too many of us do not even select books, or publicize books with any degree of sophistication. It is sad when librarians enthuse about such contemporary developments and it becomes obvious that they have never begun to understand or explore the potentiality of books.

Do many libraries impress the outsider as dynamic and contemporary organizations? Of course there are new buildings, and books in many of them look brighter than they did fifteen years ago, but on the whole libraries have an atmosphere of amiable and fusty amateurism. How many young people are likely to be inspired by the potential of librarianship on the basis of their own experience of libraries? I do believe there are some hopeful signs. Many of the younger generation of librarians have energy, enthusiasm and a broader outlook. There is even a professional journal, *The Assistant Librarian*, which runs leaders and articles on events in the outside world which are or should be relevant to librarians. What is sad is that such sound people run the risk of being crushed or becoming apathetic, if they work in dinosaur-like library systems. I have many colleagues working with children who have never been allowed to develop their potential as librarians because they are not encouraged to take responsibility or make decisions for themselves. Without the right kind of leadership, there are distinct limits to what an enthusiastic individual can do. It is no accident that the best Chief Librarians tend to attract the best staff, and also to have the most enthusiastic and helpful library committees. All of us in the profession probably know library systems we would never recommend anyone to work for, because the hierarchy are hidebound, the service stagnates, and will continue to do so. The staff will become disinterested, salaries will be low, and a ludicrously small proportion of the rates will be spent on libraries. It is often difficult to disentangle which of these disadvantages came first, but what is certain is that given one of these factors, the rest will often follow.

Even in the worst systems, children's librarians surely have nothing to lose if they try to see themselves and their work as an integrated part of the whole service? The individual librarian in a system who wants to experiment and develop the service, stands less chance than the group of librarians with this aim. It is very easy for the enthusiastic children's librarian with ideas to be ignored by a reluctant chief librarian, simply because the children's library service has come to be regarded as a separate department. If children's librarians need to be aware of the contemporary context of their work, so do all librarians. Illiteracy, poverty, reluctance to read are not problems confined to children. They can apply to a wide range of people. Libraries and librarians could have a positive role in society.

It would be inexcusably arrogant as well as crassly stupid to assume that there can be one neat philosophy of librarianship to which all public libraries should subscribe. One viewpoint is that the public library should confine itself to providing a service for those who already use it, and a strong case can be made for this, particularly in areas where a large proportion of the population are readers, and aware of the facilities offered. Such a library service, efficiently run, can make a valid contribution to the community, and maintain links with that community. But I believe that in whatever varied ways it can find to do this, a library service must not function in isolation; it must become more closely integrated into the community. I believe this, not only because I think it is possibly the only way libraries can ensure survival, but far more important, because I believe it is the way in which libraries and librarians could so truly find themselves that no one would need to query any more why libraries should exist, or what their function should be.

Only a small percentage of the public use libraries. What about the people who never come into library buildings? For many, books have lost any meaning they ever had; for many more they never had any meaning. The truth is, you can easily live without books. If librarians believe that books nevertheless offer to human beings a unique opportunity for personal development, and a uniquely individual experience for each person, surely we must try to find ways of getting more books to more people? Books are a good starting point, but the modern library service is also concerned with other materials, increasingly with every form of audio-visual aid, and also with providing information. How many of the public in any local authority area know fully what services their library provides? Traditionally libraries have been either shy or inept at publicizing the services they offer. Discreet letraset notices and booklists stencilled on duplicating paper have no impact at all, yet many libraries still rely on them for publicity. Too few library systems employ a graphic designer. Well designed and well-written publicity circulated outside libraries can help to draw attention to the scope of the service.

But inevitably, those who respond to it will tend, like most library users, to be articulate and reasonably confident people. Those who are under-privileged and inarticulate will no more venture into a public library than they will make use of any other services which are provided for the public. As social scientists must be tired of pointing out, it is always the middle classes who have the persistence and confidence to take full advantage of any legislation or organization provided theoretically for the *whole* community. Naturally this is basically a political issue, and it would be naïve to assume there is likely to be any short-term answer in a capitalist country such as ours. However, this does not mean there is *nothing* we can do, although whatever we do is bound to be limited.

Even a modern library building can appear formidable and official. Librarians are seen as Council officials, indistinguishable from rent collectors or the people in the rates office. Anyone who ventures inside, and even wants to join the library, will have to sign a form, and almost certainly give some written proof of identity. It is easy for those who have bank accounts, credit cards or driving licences; not so easy for those who cannot produce such symbols of middle class acceptability, and are also wary of signing their names and addresses on an official form. Librarians and clerical staff should always be sympathetic and understanding in such situations. But are they? I think all librarians need much more awareness of the way libraries look to the outsider. Many are plastered with prohibitive notices, and hedged about with petty regulations which seem calculated to discourage people. Of course, some librarians behave as though the last thing they want to do is to make it easy for people to use libraries anyway. There is a difference between the simple rules necessary to run a library efficiently and the complex and confusing procedures adopted in so many of them. More librarians must come to recognize this.

To make libraries more inviting is not enough. If the public won't come in, shouldn't we go out to them? The answer will depend on whether we see our role as librarians as an active or a passive one. Most of our training is concerned with such essential aspects of our work as the selection, assessment and classification of materials. We are taught how to trace materials and how to find information. This is basic and vital, and without it we should be worse than useless. However, having exercised our skills to build up collections of materials to the best of our ability, do we then just sit in our buildings waiting for the public? Are we content that so few of them ask us to use the skills we have acquired or borrow the materials we have collected? If we believe the materials we collect have value shouldn't we actively exploit them, and find ways of making them known? Shouldn't we go out and tell people about them, and about the services we offer?

I think we must, in the context of society today. It is not an easy thing to do. Traditional yardsticks of librarianship will have to be abandoned. It is common to refer to any events run by or in conjunction with a library service, other than the most basic and routine lending of materials and providing of information, as *extension activities*. In terms of *active* librarianship, this well-worn phrase is nothing more than an archaic misnomer, and should be dropped from our professional vocabulary. It implies that all such activities are additions, frills, and extras to the basic service, instead of being an integral part of it. There is always a note of caution in writing about extension activities. They seem to be generally considered a good thing, as long as there is time for them, and that they do not interfere with the proper running of the library service (which too often means librarians carrying out clerical activities which would be done by clerical staff in any efficient organization). Of course it would be nonsensical to be so involved in active librarianship that passive duties are neglected. Everything is a question of balance. I am merely making the point that everything we do should be seen as a whole, and planned as a whole. Obviously too, the terms active and passive librarianship are only used loosely. Book selection is an extremely active function.

Another often quoted dictum will have to be abandoned. There are many library systems which still measure their success by the number of books and other materials they have issued. The fact that materials have been borrowed from a library is no proof that they have been *used*. The actual figures are almost invariably inaccurate. Most of us have known individual librarians who were so insecure that they falsified issue statistics regularly, and I am sure almost unconsciously. Some library systems have got themselves into the situation where the book fund is based on issue statistics, and sometimes even on issue statistics at individual libraries. This leads to a vicious spiral, in which libraries which issue least books get least money, so the bookstock gets shabbier, and they issue even less books. It also makes librarians nervously defensive. Figures can be used to prove anything, and the arguments in relation to issue statistics are familiar. 'Our issues have gone up this year at X library, and we have had to take on more staff.' Or the favourite, 'Our issues are down this month, because the weather was so bad/good that people did not come to the library.' Issue statistics are only relevant in the most general terms, as long as it is recognized that they are almost certainly inaccurate even as a record of how many books were issued, and are certainly no kind of gauge of the *effectiveness* of the service. I believe the reluctance of many librarians to move out of libraries is their fear that even if they make some impact in the community outside, this will probably not cause the issues to go up, and therefore it will not be acknowledged as either important or valuable. Unless we can get away from the idea that our only aim is to get more people into libraries and borrowing materials, the possibilities for development are extremely limited. If we accept the idea that an important and basic part of our work is to exploit and show forth books, films, records, to people, then whether or not this results in greater borrowing is not the most relevant factor.

If librarians are to move out into the community, there will need to be staff with flexibility of outlook, sensitivity, imagination, and the willingness to experiment. Also staff who recognize that what they are doing is not an exercise in paternalism, but can be as much an expression of their professional skill as teaching is to the teacher or playing an instrument is to the musician, except that they will have been given little or no training in this aspect of their work. The field of knowledge as presented in recorded materials is so vast that it should only induce feelings of inadequacy and humility in anyone who works in a library. To venture out into the community and meet people on their own ground should induce a similar response. Provided a librarian also has a reasonable degree of personal confidence, this will be the best frame of mind in which to move out beyond the library walls.

If one thing is certain about life in the 70's, it is that in almost every area of life there is talk of breaking down barriers, and of community involvement. This is true in much educational theory, in the concepts of community schools and integrated studies; in the re-organization of social services following the Seebohm Report; in the arts in the merging of different disciplines, the development of underground culture, and in the community at large by the development of community action groups, neighbourhood councils, squatters groups. So why should libraries be different? The climate of opinion is such that whenever it is suggested that librarians should become involved and participate more in the community, even the most un-library-minded people understand immediately what is intended, and the response is sympathetic. I think that the time is ripe now. If librarians can't rouse themselves to discover ways of doing this, they could well find that the community at large will dispense with libraries to an even greater extent than it does now.

# 3
# Working Through the Community

If we believe that librarians should be more dynamic, and should move out of libraries into the communities they serve, how can this be done? There is no one answer, and no easy answer. However, I don't see how it can happen without radically altering the way so many library services operate. It certainly cannot be done unless the *entire* library service is geared to it. It is no good for a children's librarian to decide to go it alone, and work out in the community with *children*. If there is to be real involvement, then adults cannot be left out. Children do not live in isolation. The majority live with their parents, and attend clinics, schools playgroups, youth clubs, community centres run by *adults*. Nothing that relates to children can be tackled in isolation.

How can a librarian find time to get away from running a library, to spend time outside it? All of us must know branch libraries which are open for long days, say from 9.30 a.m.—8 p.m. daily, and 9.30 a.m.—5 p.m. on Saturdays. All of us know libraries which are busy, and probably even more which are not. How often is it possible to walk into small branch libraries, and find not more than half a dozen people come in during the course of an hour? How many where the branch librarian appears to be doing nothing much, or to be obviously engaged in totally non-professional tasks of a routine nature while reluctant juniors write out overdue notices?

There may be a number of reasons why some libraries are as dead as dodos. The library might be badly sited; or a change in road schemes may have rendered it virtually unapproachable; or the community it was built to serve may have moved; or even more likely, the local community may not be accustomed to reading regularly, let alone to visiting libraries and borrowing books. The long-term effect on staff in such a situation is invariably depressing. They tend gradually to slow down their rate of work until it fills the available time, giving undue importance to meaningless routines which are basically clerical anyway. The librarian becomes a kind of glorified caretaker, concerned about building repairs, the library porter's time-sheet, supervising the desk routines, rarely using even the minimum bibliographical knowledge, as most readers are regulars, with predictable and undemanding tastes in reading. Stop passers-by three streets away, ask for the nearest library, and they won't be able to direct you to it without a lot of thought.

This situation certainly used to exist in some of the libraries in Lambeth. At the same time, following the first real cutbacks in local government spending in 1966, and the sharp increase in staffing and building costs, libraries everywhere faced a crisis. It was apparent to our Director that if libraries in Lambeth continued to operate on exactly the same pattern, the service we gave would gradually but inevitably deteriorate. Also, despite the fact that he actively encouraged staff to move out into the community, most were too tied to library timetables even to begin to do this effectively. Together with the Assistant Director, he devized the comprehensive/ neighbourhood library scheme, which was instituted gradually, starting in 1970, and was to radically alter not only the service, but also its potential.

This scheme was devised to fit a particular situation in a specific area at one moment in time. I do not believe that it is possible to lay down a blueprint for a library service which would fit *any* situation. Every area is different, and has different problems. A library service which aims to serve the entire population, however difficult or impossible that may seem, cannot even begin to tackle the problem unless adjustments are made in what has been a standard pattern of running a borough library service. The only value in describing these adjustments is to show *one* way this is being done. To understand the scheme, it is necessary to know something about the area.

One of the twelve inner London boroughs (out of the total of thirty-two which make up Greater London) Lambeth has a population of 304,500. It is a multi-racial borough, predominantly West Indian, as Brixton, in the centre of the borough has traditionally been one area of London to which newly-arrived West Indians have come for over twenty years. Included among the many other nationalities are Africans, Cypriots, Poles, Indians and Pakistanis. All of which makes it a stimulating, interesting and challenging place to work. It is the second largest of the thirty-two boroughs in terms of population. Seven miles long and three miles wide at its broadest point, the borough starts on the South Bank, where are such well-known landmarks as Waterloo Station, the Old Vic (current home of the National Theatre Company), the Royal Festival Hall and the Hayward Gallery. Like most central London boroughs Lambeth is an area of contrasts. The south end of the borough is fairly suburban, the libraries busy and full of articulate readers. In other parts are all the familiar situations of any inner city—poor housing, gross overcrowding, high rise flats, interspersed with little pockets of affluence where old Georgian houses have been bought up and renovated; everywhere there is inadequate play space for children, and a distinct lack of leisure facilities; there are also over-crowded schools, and high rates of illiteracy and unemployment, particularly amongst school leavers.

There are thirteen libraries. The library service is divided into four zones. In each zone there is a *comprehensive* library, and satellite or *neighbourhood* libraries. The comprehensive library is the largest and busiest library in each zone. Take the example of West Norwood Zone. The comprehensive library is West Norwood Library and Nettlefold Hall, a large complex, opened in 1969. It is open weekdays from 9.30 a.m.—8 p.m., Saturdays 9.30 a.m.—6 p.m., and gives a full service to the public, lending materials (that is, books, records, cassettes and other audio-visual aids), and answering reference enquiries. It also has eleven study carrels for students, and a language laboratory. The total bookstock is about 70,000 volumes. The other libraries in the zone are the Carnegie Library, Herne Hill, and the St. Martin's Library, Tulse Hill. The former is a solid building, architecturally designed in the same style as all the libraries endowed by Andrew Carnegie, and isolated in a sedately residential area, a quarter of a mile from Herne Hill shopping centre; the latter is a distinctly unappealing small, modern library, built into the ground floor of a housing estate. These two libraries are designated as the neighbourhood libraries for the zone. This means that their aim is to serve the least mobile people in the community—

that is, children, mothers with young children, and old people. They carry smaller and more popular stocks than the comprehensive library, and the stock will be completely changed from time to time. They are not open for such long hours as the comprehensive library. Their pattern of opening times, based on a traffic survey of the area, is two days 11 a.m.—6 p.m., two days 3 p.m.—8 p.m., Saturdays 9 a.m.—5 p.m., and one weekday closed. Everyone in the area of these two neighbourhood libraries is not much more than a mile from the comprehensive library at West Norwood. The neighbourhood libraries are being converted so that they can be fully used by the community at all times. In the case of St. Martin's Library, which was formerly an open-plan one-room branch, with the children's library on one side of the entrance, the adult library on the other, the entire stock has been moved into one half of the building. The other half has been screened off, and turned into an activities room, which is let to organizations including Centre '70, a very active local Community Association. A pre-school playgroup run by the association meets there on several weekday mornings. It is hoped eventually to have this room fully used throughout the day for community activities and meetings, including of course, any events organized by the librarians in that zone.

The comprehensive/neighbourhood scheme was started as an experiment in the Central Zone in September 1970, and was confirmed as viable in October, 1971. By 1974 the other three zones will have changed to this system as well, although the opening times of the neighbourhood libraries in each zone will not be the same, because it is recognized that the needs of each zone are different, since each area of the borough is strikingly different.

There are no longer any branch librarians in Lambeth, because there are no longer any branch libraries. The zone is instead the basic unit. There is a Zone Librarian who heads the staff in each zone. Librarians are no longer based at one service point. Instead they have become part of a team responsible for working in a zone. They move around, and are on duty at the different service points in the zone, but they are also much freer to work in the community, and a vital part of their responsibility is to build up a detailed knowledge of the community within which they operate in the zone.

For the first time they are able to work as fully professional librarians, dividing their time between such activities as stock control, reader's advice at different service points, and working in the community to develop awareness of the library service. This would not have been possible just by radically altering library opening hours, and treating staff as a team working in an area instead of being based at individual libraries. An essential part of the scheme has been the appointment of clerical staff, known as Continuity Assistants, who are responsible for the day to day running of neighbourhood libraries, and also for supervising routines at comprehensive libraries. In the neighbourhood libraries, the continuity assistant is on duty most of the time a library is open, and is responsible for opening up and locking the building, supervising the shelving and issuing of books, the checking of reservations, reporting building repairs, filling in statistical and other forms, and all other routines which too often are carried out by librarians. Clerical staff, many of them part-time, are employed to carry out all the counter routines. Apart from the fact the librarians are freed from clerical routines, the great advantage is that these routines are supervised by people specially selected for their competence in such matters. Inevitably, they tend to be much better at doing this kind of work than librarians who quite reasonably regarded these duties as nothing to do with librarianship, although they are essential to make librarianship effective.

A team of librarians works in a zone, and it is assumed that all of them are able to carry out any professional duties, just because they are qualified librarians. We have abandoned the idea of full-time specialists amongst the zone staff. The team in each zone are all either 'librarians' or 'senior librarians' according to their position. However most of them will specialize, for example in music or reference services, or work with children or young adults, but this will only be for part of their time. How does this operate as far as the library service to children is concerned? The only full-time specialists in children's work are the Children's Librarian and the Assistant Children's librarian, although as will become apparent, the scope of our job is much wider than our designation implies anyway. In each zone staff will find themselves coming into contact with children at times, particularly when on duty as the only librarian at one of the neighbourhood libraries. There are staff who will be more deeply involved in working with children. Some of them will only take part in one specific activity, for example, pre-school story-telling. They will be given a short training, and will then visit several pre-school organizations for storytelling each week. Others will take part in the full range of activities, including book selection, stock revision, visits to local organizations and storytelling. Some will work with children for an average of perhaps one day out of five, and others for four days out of five. Zone staff are responsible to their Zone Librarian, but those involved in children's work are also functionally responsible to the Children's Librarian.

Not surprisingly, this system means that staff with a wide range of abilities, talents and experience are participating in children's work. Many who would never have considered being involved if this had meant a full-time commitment, are prepared to spend part of their time in this way. How refreshing it is, for example, to have staff with a good knowledge of the adult bookstock bringing their experience to bear on selecting children's books. Inevitably attitudes to children amongst librarians who formerly ignored them are changing, and I find it very amusing as well as encouraging that people who used to be vociferous about their total lack of interest in 'children's librarianship' are beginning to show enthusiasm for some of our projects with children. Once staff attitudes begin to change, this also affects the way the libraries operate. There used to be many differences in Lambeth between a child and an adult using the library. Why, they even had different coloured tickets and registration forms! Everything has been brought into line, so that whether you are nine or ninety, there is no difference in the way you join the library or the number of items you borrow. In all the neighbourhood libraries where this is geographically possible, the children's stock is housed in the same room as the adult stock, which removes those artificial barriers which used to prevent adults from going into the 'children's library' and children into the 'adult library'.

Our comprehensive/neighbourhood system is very new, and very flexible. Many changes in detail are sure to happen over the next few years. The scheme pre-supposes a more comprehensive programme of in-service training for *all* librarians in *all* aspects of librarianship than we have yet managed to achieve. It is only now that the scheme is operating that some of the training needs are becoming apparent, but I think most of us in Lambeth are convinced that the service is at least *beginning* to develop along the most helpful lines for our particular situation. It must be obvious that librarians have to be very flexible and adaptable in their attitudes to work in the zone system. One Zone Librarian has said that she thought it took her staff about a year to adjust psychologically to not being based at one library, and also to being relieved of routine duties which used to take up so much time. There is no doubt that most of the staff have responded enthusiastically to the new system. It has led generally to a broadening of outlook and a widening of horizons, simply because staff are both free to move around outside libraries, and also because they are not marooned at *one* library. Instead of some staff being rushed off their feet at busy service points, whilst others became bored at quiet ones, everyone now regularly experiences different libraries. It is true too, that the neighbourhood libraries, open shorter hours, are much livelier and busier than before. Inevitably, staff develop a broader outlook in every respect. The parochial attitudes which many frequently suffered from—the inability to see beyond their own library and feel themselves to be part of the entire library service—are disappearing. So are the little idiosyncratic differences in practice which used to be apparent to those of us who visited all the libraries! Instead of a detailed knowledge of books and readers at one service point, staff have an admittedly more sketchy experience of readers at a group of libraries, and also of the different bookstocks in their zone. The effect on book selection is marked. Instead of one person interpreting the needs at one service point in relation to that bookstock, several staff select books together for a group of libraries, based on their joint experience.

This system rightly raises many questions in relation to work with children. I can envisage that many children's librarians would resist it totally. Probably the most obvious question is: Won't children miss the attention of one individual children's librarian they can get to know, who will nearly always (with the exception of

times off duty) be there? I would never under-estimate the value
of this to a child who uses the library. My experience as a practising
children's librarian was in such a situation, but it is never as perfect
as its protagonists claim. How late are children's libraries open on
weekdays? According to replies to a Library Association questionnaire in 1968, almost twice as many children's libraries stayed open
until 7 p.m. or later as closed at 6.30 p.m. or earlier. On how many of
those five nights would a children's librarian be likely to be on duty
until 7 p.m. or later? Probably two, possibly three, most unlikely to
be more than three? And how about Saturdays? How many Saturdays do children's librarians have off duty? One in three? One in
four? Alternative Saturdays? Conditions of service vary in different
authorities, but it must be obvious that there will be many times
when the children's librarian based at one service point is not on
duty when the children's library is open. So, who *is* on duty?
Another children's librarian? In some cases, maybe. But there are
not likely to be many authorities with more than one children's
librarian per branch. A trainee? Possibly. A junior member of staff?
Undoubtedly the most likely. Already it is not such a perfect situation as is often depicted. How about the children who *don't* come
into the library? Is it right that those who use the library should
have the privilege of getting to know one children's librarian who is
often there and able to give them individual attention, whilst
children who possibly have more need to know about the library
service have much less chance of meeting a children's librarian? It
seems to me a very basic and crucial question. Are we content to
give a superb service to children who come into the library? Or do
we think we have as much responsibility towards children *outside*
the library? Is our brief to serve *some* children or the *total* child
population?

In Lambeth we have no doubts about the answer to that question,
although we are only just beginning to face up to the implications of
such a challenge. How does one move out into the community? I
want to make two things clear. One is that other libraries are doing
many of the things I shall talk about that we are attempting in
Lambeth. The other is that our library service has been re-organized
to make more involvement in the community possible. Essentially

this applies to every aspect of the library service, and it is important
to bear in mind that my comments about work with children should
always be seen in this wider context. It would be equally valid and
interesting to examine the effect of the comprehensive/neighbour-
hood system on work with old and housebound people, or on the
expansion of the Lambeth Information Network (LINK) which
aims to provide specialist information to business firms in the
borough.

For library purposes, if it is necessary to define a child, our
Lambeth definition is any person between the ages of one to about
twelve. I should like to consider in detail how we are trying to
tackle our responsibilities towards the pre-school child. We believe
that librarians should move out into the community, but also that
collections of books should too. Books should be where people are.
There are currently over ninety organizations specifically concerned
with the pre-school child in Lambeth. They include about seventy
pre-school playgroups. Some are orthodox, some unorthodox; some
are run by organizations like the Elfrida Rathbone Society and the
Save the Children Fund; some belong to the Pre-School Playgroup
Association, some don't. Then there are privately run nursery
groups. The variations can be bewildering. What is refreshing about
being a librarian is that we need not concern ourselves with the
differences. All of them need books, and do not have money for
books and we are the book-providing authority. All of them borrow
about twenty books at a time, and change them whenever they like.
We also lend books to the day nurseries which look after pre-school
children of working mothers; to the child health centres which run
crèches for young children whose mothers are visiting the clinic;
and to the One O'Clock Clubs. I consider the latter to be one of the
most interesting of the developments in care for pre-school children.
Pioneered by the Greater London Council, (GLC) in parks throughout London, the first One O'Clock Club opened in Brockwell Park,
Lambeth, in April 1965. Each club is equipped with a rudimentary
hut, and a fenced off outdoor area, with facilities for creative play.
The clubs, run by trained supervisors, open at 1 p.m. every weekday
until 4.30 p.m. throughout the year, except for Bank Holidays. Any
mother with a pre-school child is welcome, but they must stay with

their children and not just leave them. The clubs become an important meeting place for young mothers, and do a great deal to relieve the loneliness and isolation felt by so many of those living in high rise flats.

We found that some people were initially nervous about borrowing library books for such groups. Because the books are in good condition, they sometimes still get treated as sacred objects and locked away, to be brought out on special occasions for children to look at under strict supervision. This is hardly the way to encourage children to *enjoy* books, which is, after all, the object of the exercise. They should be left around, so that small children can learn to browse. Books are to be used. That is what they are for. Naturally young children have to be taught how to turn pages without tearing them and so on, but this can be done casually in the context of a group. Inevitably if young children enjoy books, they will become battered and dirty, and the majority of them will probably have to be discarded on return to the library. Librarians should be suspicious if books are returned from such groups in mint condition.

It is paradoxical that the increasingly sophisticated and lavishly produced full-colour picture book is more counter-productive than many publishers seem to realize. Faced by books of such obvious 'quality', people who are not used to handling them feel nervous, and the view that books are in some way rarified and special is reinforced. Small wonder that the instinctive reaction of adults to a collection of picture books can be that they are too good to be handled by children. Librarians often have to fight hard to counteract this view when lending collections to organizations. Many picture books are in danger of becoming the equivalent of coffee-table books for adults, seen as a prestige luxury item rather than as a necessity. Picture books last for such a short time even in the hands of the most careful children, and this is another reason people are sometimes wary of them. I would not deny that there is a place for beautiful and lavish books, but it would be refreshing to see also books which have a more common touch. Some of the most successful and long-lasting early picture books like Wanda Gag's *Millions of Cats* or Marie Hall Ets's *In the Forest* had only black and white illustrations. Such books are unlikely to be produced today. There is a related problem. Picture books are used mainly to read to and look at with young children, and also for them to pore over by themselves. Despite the abundance of books which are beautiful to look at, the number with texts short enough and good enough to read to children under six is extremely small, and if retellings of traditional tales like *The Old Woman and her Pig* are excluded, is tiny indeed. Obviously it is easier to find artists excited by the scope of picture book illustration than it is to find writers who want to accept the challenge and limitations of writing texts for such books. However, nothing would please the increasingly large numbers of people working with young children and interested in books for them than to see rather fewer 'beautiful' picture books, and rather more which may look less stunning, but have totally convincing and readable texts. Small wonder that when visiting pre-school organizations it is quite common to find that the staff there have more or less abandoned picture books for storytelling, and are to be seen using books written as 'easy readers' for this purpose, which is a great pity.

Books should be where people are. The impact of books in pre-school playgroups has been tremendous, as the many library systems which lend them must have discovered. It is hard to understand how any authority can refuse to supply them, but many do. Just as there are some library systems which for some incomprehensible reason have chosen to believe that library legislation only empowers them to provide books for children of seven and over (that is, those more than half of whose childhood has gone), so some authorities will undoubtedly hold out on providing books for playgroups. Their attitude is typified by a librarian of a large authority with whom I discussed this question heatedly some years ago. He said: 'This pre-school playgroup wrote to me, and asked if they could borrow twenty books. I thought about it, and I realized that if I said "Yes", in a short time there could be two hundred playgroups, then where should I be?' The answer is that he might have been providing an invaluable service. He would certainly be giving all playgoup children the opportunity of handling more books than could otherwise be provided; also possibly getting books to children who would not otherwise see many until they started school, already irretrievably handicapped in their development and so in their educational opportunities. It is not necessary to labour the point about the importance of the first five years of life, when attention is drawn to it at least once a week in the national press in comments about child development, Educational Priority Areas, and cultural deprivation. If the point still hasn't got through, and a sense of urgency communicated to librarians who should be in a position to make a contribution towards enriching the experience of young children, then this is just another sad comment on the blinkered outlook of our profession.

Our librarians visit pre-school organizations of every kind for picture book storytelling sessions. There are several reasons why we think this is more satisfactory than bringing groups to the library for storytelling. Very young children come to recognize the librarian as part of their environment, and as someone whose visits they associate with the enjoyment of listening to stories. As a three-year-old remarked to a librarian visiting a group for the first time, 'Oh, are you the library today?' The librarian is seen to be as much at home in the playgroup as the children themselves. It also gives librarians an invaluable opportunity to meet both staff and mothers on their homeground, which undoubtedly helps to develop a greater awareness of the context in which other people are seeing children. It is also an encouragement to some mothers to go and visit a library with their children, if they have met a librarian informally first and have established how simple it is to borrow books. It is therefore important to meet not only pre-school children, but the adults who look after them, because the child under five is almost entirely dependent on adults. We give talks on children's books and reading to the course run locally for pre-school playgroup supervisors; to a course at one of the evening institutes for mothers of young children; to groups of students from the local college of Further Education who are training as housemothers and nursery nurses; to any groups of mothers from Young Wives groups (and grandmothers groups) at local churches; to mothers attached to playgroups who meet informally in their homes; to refresher courses run for health visitors and child health centre superintendents; and most recently, talks specifically on storytelling to day nursery staff who have heard our staff telling stories in day nurseries and want to do so themselves.

There is no bookshop in Lambeth where it is possible to see even a small collection of good children's books. A great deal of interest in books has been generated amongst mothers and those working with young children over the past ten years in this country alongside interest in all other matters relating to their early growth and development. Since 1970 we have mounted an annual exhibition, *The First Seven Years*, which features selected books for children up to the age of seven published during the previous year. The first two years the exhibition stayed in one place, but by 1972 we decided it was absurd for our exhibitions to be static, when books were moving around all over the borough. The exhibition opened in March, and toured until November, by which time it had been on show at twenty-two different sites. These included health centres, leisure centres, community centres and a one night stand at the AGM of the Inner London Pre-School Playgroup Association, which happened to be held in the borough. The exhibition was aimed at adults rather than children, and so was sent to places parents and people working with young children might be expected to visit. For a week it was housed in a white-painted double-decker bus outside Waterloo Station to attract commuters (mainly fathers) who pour out of the station daily to work in Lambeth.

We are only at the beginning of the possibilities as far as pre-school children and books are concerned. Obviously we don't have enough staff to do regular storytelling in more than approximately two thirds of the pre-school organizations. We hope to extend this by involving students from our two local Colleges of Education. We plan to train them in storytelling, so that they can take part in the programme, which we hope will also be a valuable experience for them. There are currently at least 600 childminders registered with the Council, and we are exploring the best way of getting books to them, because they look after a large number of pre-school children. In addition to the mobile library starting shortly, which will operate through the different zones, we hope one day to buy a double-decker bus to use for a pre-school programme. The bus will be equipped for films and storytelling, whilst the lower deck will carry books for children and adults, so that we can tour around and meet some of the children who do not go to any pre-school group and their mothers. This idea has come from two sources: our use of a bus at Waterloo Station, and an account of a similar pre-school programme in Queensborough Public Library, New York, which I heard about when visiting New York in the autumn of 1971. What is most exciting about all this, is that once you begin to make contacts, you don't have to think of all the ideas. They will develop naturally from the contacts. The idea of *The First Seven Years* came from the staff of the then Health Department in Lambeth. I have used the example of the pre-school child to illustrate how contacts can develop with a limited but fairly compact and easily defined group of children. The same principles can be applied to all children—in fact to all people.

There has been another important development in Lambeth which has helped to clarify and consolidate what we are trying to do in the library service. In July 1970, all Council departments were re-organized, and nine Directorates were created. The Libraries Department became the Directorate of Amenity Services. The former Chief Librarian, Roy McColvin was appointed Director. The Directorate has two divisions, Libraries and Recreation, with an Assistant Director for each division. The Recreation Division is responsible for the sports centres, swimming pools, organized activities in parks (as opposed to maintenance, which is the responsibility of another Directorate), play spaces, One O'Clock Clubs, leisure centres, and all cultural and recreational activities organized by the Council. For us this is a tremendously exciting development. When the Directorate was established it was made quite clear that the two divisions were not to see themselves as separate entities, but should place no limits on their thinking about ways of co-operating and working together. The logic of combining all services connected with leisure seems to me inescapable. Nothing is more salutary than being forced to consider the needs of the library service in such close juxtaposition to other leisure needs of the local community. There is no better way of learning to see one's own work in perspective. In a system which has no clear-cut policy, this kind of alignment of services could obviously appear as a threat. However, the importance of the library service is not in question. But nor is the need for more pools, for leisure centres with a wide range of activities, or play areas for children. Funds are not limitless, and extremely difficult choices have to be made about expenditure. It is a necessary discipline to re-examine continually and ruthlessly everything one does in the light of this knowledge.

This development has helped immeasurably to extend our horizons. What better place than a sports centre for children's books? The largest and best equipped is the Ferndale Sports Centre in Brixton, used by people of all ages for a wide range of activities. In the school holidays large numbers of young people between the ages of five to fifteen are likely to be there. They don't want to play any sport all day long, but many of them visit the centre for hours at a time, just as many children stay in libraries for hours during the holidays. After a game of football, they are likely to go to the canteen for a drink of squash, where they will find a collection of books from the library. They are often youngsters who would be unlikely to visit a library, and probably wouldn't sit down and browse if they did. However, relaxing in the sports centre after an energetic game is different, and many of them in fact *do* look at books. They can borrow them to take home without even signing a form, and some do. The staff there have a supply of library registration forms, and it is easy for them to suggest casually to children who show some interest in books that they might like to join the library up the road. I am quite sure that some children who might not accept such a suggestion from a librarian will do so if it comes from a person they admire as a sportsman, who does not have any obvious incentive in encouraging them to read.

Pools, too, are good places for books. At the moment there is nowhere to accommodate permanent collections at the two indoor and two outdoor pools, but this will change. There was a display of children's paperbacks at Clapham Pool during National Book Week in 1972. There is no doubt too that pools are ideal sites for the kind of comprehensive exhibitions we have organized in the past in Lambeth like the Children's Book Festivals, described in detail in a later chapter. Each summer the sites for our outdoor storytelling programme include many places within the Directorate like the play spaces, parks, sports centres and one of the outdoor pools. The fact that we know the staff and the way such places are organized is a tremendous help. What becomes increasingly obvious is that it makes sense to plan and work together, because everything we do is closely inter-related. We are all concerned with the same children in different situations, and to compare notes can be extremely helpful. I often look back to the days when we worked inside the library almost exclusively, and apart from contacts with schools, had no way of meeting groups of children. We worried about those children who spent hours aimlessly in the library in the school holidays; or about those who came in to try and do their homework in a busy library because there was nowhere else to go; or about individual children or groups who invariably made their presence felt and disrupted everyone; meanwhile, at the sports centres, the pools and the parks, the staff there were thinking the same things about the same children! All of us are concerned with providing opportunities for the enjoyment of leisure—doesn't it make sense to work together? I have met librarians who regard the alignment of services in this way as a retrograde step—and one which they imply is slightly demeaning for libraries. This seems to me to be utter nonsense. To say that we are concerned with leisure activities is to be concerned with a vital aspect of life, and one to which an increasing amount of time will be devoted in the near future. People read for a hundred reasons, and to call reading a leisure activity does not exclude reading for information, education, cultural development, general enlightenment, or any of those loaded words usually trotted out to justify the existence of libraries. We should never forget that reading is just *one* activity people can enjoy. The man who *only* reads is a limited human being indeed. Libraries have begun to develop from such a narrow concept by recognizing that their responsibilities extend beyond the lending of books to the lending of records, tapes, cassettes, slides, pictures, films and so on; and to the recognition that libraries should not only passively lend materials, but should also actively exploit them. Many libraries are now closely linked with their local arts associations. Because Lambeth Council decided to amalgamate all recreational activities in one Directorate, it is made much easier for us to think of the total picture in everything that we do. Every time we have a new idea, it is becoming automatic to think about who else should be involved or could help us. Will it relate to the activities of Lambeth Arts and Recreations Association (LARA)? Could the play spaces be involved? The logic seems to us increasingly sound, and gives a new dimension to everything that we do.

So far, I have not mentioned one major organization concerned with children: schools. Much has been written about public library/school relationships in authorities which are responsible for both services, and the fruitful ways in which the service can be integrated. Lambeth, as one of the twelve boroughs which make up Inner London, is not responsible for the school library service, which is run by the Inner London Education Authority (ILEA), and so my comments relate specifically to this type of situation. There are ILEA library advisors for school libraries, and we have always worked closely and discussed common problems with the advisor for the Lambeth area, as well as consulting before we make changes in policy which might affect the schools. At the moment secondary schools with over 1,200 pupils can employ a full-time librarian, and those with less pupils a qualified part-time librarian. The staff in each zone in Lambeth are responsible for maintaining contact with the schools in their area, as with all other organizations. Schools are visited regularly, and our librarians are sometimes asked to give talks to individual classes or to the whole school. Many teachers make full use of our libraries, and we also lend collections of books for specific school projects, provided reasonable notice is given. Teachers in London have several sources on which to draw for projects as well as their own school library. They can use the Media Resources Centre at Highbury for reference purposes and borrow materials from the Education Library at County Hall, and also from their local public library. We do not, however, lend block loans of books to schools as some inner London libraries do, as I believe it is the responsibility of ILEA to ensure that school libraries are adequately stocked. At a meeting of Senior London Children's Librarians in 1971, attended by the Principal Organizer of the ILEA Library Services, Richard Mainwood, several librarians commented that they felt schools were making too great demands on them for books. As Mr. Mainwood pointed out, the public libraries of inner London are under no obligation whatsoever to lend books to schools. Despite this, most of us are anxious to do what we can within reasonable limits. Years ago, before the school library services had developed fully, Lambeth, like many other London boroughs, encouraged teachers to bring the same class of children on regular visits to the libraries, changing their books on each visit. At that time, this exercise served a useful purpose, as there were not enough books in schools anyway, and large numbers of children would never have found the library on their own. The most dedicated teachers made the most of these visits, and encouraged their children in every way, but the less enthusiastic ones clearly saw the visits as a convenient free period for themselves, once the children were deposited in the library. I would not deny that some children were helped by this scheme, but the most telling time was at the end of the school term, when the majority of the children, seeing the library visits as a school activity, handed their tickets in until the end of the holidays. In modern terms, such visits seem purposeless, and this scheme was abandoned some years ago, with the full agreement of ILEA school library service, as they too felt that it was neither an intelligent nor a contemporary way to introduce children to public libraries.

We prefer to encourage primary schools to send each class in the school about once a year, rather than arranging more frequent visits for one class. Over the past fifteen years, one of the events to which most schools have responded has been the annual Children's Book Festival, which involved an exhibition of books and related materials at each branch library, and also visits by authors and artists, as well as speakers on the theme of the exhibition. We have been extremely grateful for the support and enthusiasm of teachers for this event over the years. The annual Book Festival is changing as we adjust to the comprehensive/neighbourhood system, and it is possible that in future each zone might arrange an annual exhibition which would be flexible enough to be mounted at different times in the year at each individual library in the zone, as well as at other Directorate buildings in the area. This it is hoped will then continue to provide the focal point for most of the class visits. This system has always

*Above:* Gathering an audience for storytelling on a housing estate

*Below:* Housing estate storytelling session

Books in a
sports centre
© *Will Green*

worked well as far as Book Festivals are concerned, and the majority of primary schools and a fair proportion of the junior classes of secondary schools have visited the libraries for a dual-purpose visit—to see the exhibition or attend a talk, and to be reminded about the library services. I don't think school class visits to libraries on non-festive occasions serve much valuable purpose, except in the case of the youngest children, or for older children who can be shown something of the entire resources of the library service. I cannot accept the value of making visits to the public library an occasion for 'lessons' on how to use reference books or the catalogue. At least there is never any chance of the latter in Lambeth, as we don't have catalogues in children's libraries, the reasons for which will be explained in a later chapter. Comments about how to join the library, or what to do if you have lost a book, or want to reserve one, can be easily made at the end of a visit for some other purpose without appearing too didactic. Children need to know at an increasingly early age how to find facts, or how to extract information once found, but a class visit to a public library is not the best situation for this to be put across. I feel the same way about set book talks to school classes in the public library. This activity, almost invariably inflicted on a group of children the librarian does not know well, or has never met before at any rate as a group, is probably fairly meaningless. And here we come to what I feel to be the most important difference between the two complementary services in schools and public libraries. The school librarian and the teacher interested in books have a very specific responsibility. Working within a defined community, with the opportunity to get to know a small number of children well, it is possible to give a truly *individual* service; to know well not only those children who attend the school, but also to follow the development of their reading tastes. I say a 'small number of children' advisedly, although in the case of a large comprehensive school, the total number of young people could hardly be called small. However, it is small compared with the number for which the public library has to take responsibility. It is estimated currently that the population of Lambeth ages one to fourteen is 58,990. The largest comprehensive school in the borough has 1,600 pupils. The school librarian and the teacher can do a tremendous amount to encourage reading just because they are in a situation which enables them to work with the same small group in more depth than the librarian in the public library. Admittedly this opportunity is not always seized. Just as there are imaginative and conscientious librarians, and also lazy ones with limited horizons and rigidity of outlook, so is the same true of teachers. Those who are good can have a startling effect on the reading of the children they teach, and this should never be under-estimated. Here is the ideal situation for book talks, and supremely for reading books aloud—to a group well known to the teacher. Unfortunately many teachers are woefully ignorant about children's books. I have some-times talked to students in Colleges of Education about encouraging children to read, and have become aware that what I am saying is meaningless, because the students have never themselves found enjoyment in reading.

Obviously the school library should be geared to the teaching needs of the school, and it is this area that the school most frequently wants supplementary material from the public library. Unfortunately here too, problems arise. Libraries are bombarded with requests for non-existent books from children prompted by teachers who have not considered it necessary to acquaint themselves with the bibliography of a subject before embarking on a project. It is sad when this happens, because co-operation with teachers who do prepare their subjects well is extremely fruitful. My own reserva-tions about the frenzied excitement over the establishment of school library resource centres springs not from animosity towards audio-visual aids, which can be extremely valuable, but from a fear that many of the people who are getting involved in them have still not learned how to use properly those rather old-fashioned aids, books.

In Lambeth we have always been very pleased that despite the fact our relationship is a voluntary one, most schools in the borough welcome co-operation with us. The schools are hard-pressed, frequently over-crowded and under-staffed, and we try never to forget this when making approaches to them. The main reason, years ago, that we first produced succinct publicity leaflets announc-ing details of the Children's Book Festival to take on school visits, was to save the time of the headteachers who had little to spare. To spend fifteen minutes in the office of any primary school head is to realize something of what teachers in an urban area like Lambeth have to cope with in the course of a day. Interruptions from children, teachers, parents and other visitors are incessant. The range of problems the head has to deal with is staggering. Although incredibly, many of them manage to know and spend time with parents, the euphoric concept of the 'community school' (with the school as a focal point, drawing adults within its walls for extra-curricular activities, and itself reaching out to participate in the whole life of the local community) is a long way off.

It is certainly true that there has been a change of emphasis in our relationship with schools in Lambeth. There was a time when the only way we made contact with groups of children was through the schools. This is no longer true. Schools are just one of the organizations concerned with children with whom we keep in touch. Our own responsibilities have become clearer in recent years as we have begun to move out into the community, and have perhaps been finally clarified by the creation of the Directorate. Although the work and responsibilities of teachers obviously cannot be defined in this way, children are actually *in* school on 200 of the 365 days in the year. When they are in school, the school library and the school librarian and the teacher provide for their reading needs, and the public librarian should concentrate a large proportion of the time on pre-school children. In the evenings, at weekends and in the school holidays, the public librarian may well concentrate more on school age children, and give less time to the pre-school group. This seems to me a fair way of looking at the responsibility librarians in authorities like Lambeth should accept. The rest of the Directorate too, is concerned mainly with children out of school, and we shall work closer together as time goes on. We do not see the child in isolation, and so many of our programmes as they develop will see the child in the context of the family and of the whole community. Our relationship with schools has changed, but it is still a vital one, and will undoubtedly develop in new ways, as schools are changing too. However, the days when we needed class visits almost more than they needed us (if only to show we were able to get children into libraries and meet them in groups, rather

than relying on their haphazard and voluntary appearance within
our walls) have gone.

It is reasonable that an outsider may not appreciate the distinction
there can be in the two types of service in public libraries and school
libraries, and may see it only as wasteful duplication. This was
obviously the reaction of those who compiled the *Report of the
Commissioner of Education's Committee on Library Development*
published by the State Education Department of the State of New
York in 1970. This report was being widely discussed when I
visited New York late in 1971. It states:

> In general it may be said that school libraries, or library media centres, in
> New York State range from those which are little more than token collections to
> those which are physically and educationally the centre of the entire teaching
> and learning experience. In schools with limited resources, students usually
> depend on the public library to meet their library requirements . . . In New
> York State, 700 independent public libraries serve, with varying degrees of
> adequacy, what can be considered for all practical purposes the entire population
> of the State.

. . . and goes on to say:

> The primary mission of school, college and special libraries is clear enough
> (to support the efforts of the institutions which maintain them), but public
> libraries suffer to some extent from a lack of clarity about what exactly their role
> in society ought to be.

Without going into the full ramifications of the report (which
should be compulsory reading for all school and public librarians in
this country), the committee arrives at the bureaucratically neat
conclusion that:

> The elementary school media centre should have the responsibility and
> capacity to meet all the library needs of all children except those in health,
> welfare, and correctional institutions.

Naturally this suggestion caused a ferment amongst librarians.
Children's librarians in public libraries were outraged at the suggestion that they should no longer be responsible for providing a
service to children. Their reactions were understandably defensive,
because the justification for their whole professional existence was

being questioned. Three articles in *Library Journal* (15th October 1971) *Patterns of Children's Library Service in New York State* reflect some of the most important arguments generated by the report. Dorothy Broderick, in a characteristically pungent article, commented that there were sure to be librarians in both school and public libraries who thought the report had nothing to do with them, and how wrong they were. Her remarks could equally well apply to us here.

Although so many of the things which happen in Lambeth are made easier or possible because of the comprehensive/neighbour-hood set-up, and because we work within a Directorate concerned with every aspect of leisure, much of it develops from the way we are learning to *think* about work. Many of the things that happen involve no extra staffing, no expenditure, but they do require thought. And any librarian can think. Our Director is known for his aphorisms. One of the most often quoted is 'I don't want anything happening in the borough where our name isn't mentioned' and it is a good one to bear in mind all the time. After all, it is hardly news that people working in different disciplines are trying to break down barriers, and recognize the inter-relation between the work so many of us do in the community. Libraries are only following a long-established lead in doing this.

It is hardly surprising that I am able to justify the existence of a Children's Librarian and an Assistant Children's Librarian to co-ordinate the services to children in a borough like Lambeth. Obviously part of our work is to supervise the teams of staff in the four zones who are spending part of their time with children; to arrange in-service training in children's work at different levels; to co-ordinate and control book selection and stock revision; to meet regularly with our colleagues at all levels to discuss improvements in what we are already doing, and future plans. Our concern should always be policy rather than practice. Obviously there will be consultation about changes in practice, for example the way the reservations system works, and part of our responsibility is to see that the system *does* work. There is no need for us to be deeply involved in the details once they have been agreed. Matters like the mechanics of book ordering are so organized that the only thing we have to do is decide or confirm *which* books are to be ordered. The rest is clerical, or the responsibility of those concerned with cataloguing and classification of books. The most important thing we do is to plan, innovate and enlarge our contacts with other people. Most ideas develop naturally.

Last summer, the outdoor storytelling team arrived for the first session at a temporary play space. It proved a very unsuitable site for various reasons, and on the spur of the moment they transferred the session to a large open tree-lined area in the middle of a housing estate. This worked, and adults came out on balconies to listen. We realized that we had not begun to consider the possibilities of storytelling on housing estates, but had tended to concentrate on parks, open spaces and sports centres. Before planning routes for this summer, we talked to the Directorate of Housing about the programme, and asked for their help in choosing the most isolated estates where children had least chance of getting to a park or open space. The area housing managers discussed this, and came up with a list. We spent a day touring with them round the possible sites, and then made a final choice. They were very helpful in giving us contacts on each estate, and also helping to arrange for the distribution of leaflets announcing storytelling sessions. These sites turned out to be extremely interesting as well as challenging and proved a most important development in our storytelling programme, which has opened up all kinds of possibilities for the future.

We began to talk about the possibility of touring *The First Seven Years* exhibition while involved in selecting the books for the 1972 exhibition. (There is so much work involved in selecting books and mounting an exhibition, that it does not make sense to put it on in just one place for a short time.) We thought of all the most obvious places. We asked the Directorate of Health and Protection if any of the child health centres would be interested in having the exhibition. The answer came back, nearly all of them. Waterloo Station too, seemed a good possible site, but proved too complicated and costly at £230 for a week. However, we were offered another site, which had never been tried out, at the bottom of the steps leading down from the main station exit. The problem was to find something in which to house the exhibition. The answer was a double-decker bus which our Directorate of Civil Engineering and Public Services use for public safety exhibitions. They were extremely helpful, and keen to lend us the bus. The only problem was that the site still cost about half as much as the site on the station, which of course we could not afford. However, remembering that publishers pay for their books to be on display for National Book League exhibitions, we approached the Children's Book Group of the Publisher's Association, to see if the publishers whose books we had selected would be prepared to pay £1 for each of their books in the exhibition. The response was enthusiastic, and everyone agreed. Always we have been tremendously impressed, in whatever we do, by the enthusiasm of the people we approach for help. The staff at Waterloo Station could not have been more constructive, from telling us where to fill our kettle with water, to ingeniously rigging up an electric cable from their office window down to the bus via a lamp-post fitted with a power point into which we plugged. From this followed the idea of a bus of our own, because we had learned from a London Transport visitor to the bus that they are sold off cheaply after fifteen years service. So many people are now using buses for mobile pre-school playgroups that we are trying to visit most of them before deciding how our bus needs to be fitted out. We are working closely on this idea with our Directorate of Social Service, because of their deep involvement in work with pre-school children, as well as talking to everyone else who might be interested.

The *Guardian* started a campaign about holiday activities for children, and the general scarcity of information about what is being done in any specific area. We had not advertised our first major outdoor storytelling programme in 1970 much, and felt that we should do more in 1971. The Directorate was still very new, and few people in the community at large knew much about it. Perhaps we should compile a leaflet about Directorate activities for children in the summer holidays? It seemed silly to stop at Directorate activities. So we produced the first issue of *What's on for Children in and around Lambeth*; *Summer Holidays 1971*. We tried to find out all activities, events and places children could visit during the holidays. We phoned every organization and individual we knew, and one contact led to another. Our mailing list doubled; and we

were able to talk about what we are trying to do to many people we
had never come across before. The guide proved one of the most
useful and successful things we had ever produced. Ten thousand
free copies disappeared in the first three weeks of the holidays. In
1972, the guide increased in size, as inevitably we had missed out a
number of organizations the first time, and also more things were
happening. The inclusion of a map of Lambeth with all sites
marked proved invaluable, and adults as well as children could be
seen clutching them everywhere in the borough. This is such an
*easy* thing to do, and once done, it is obviously easier the second
time. Why don't more libraries do it?

So, librarians move out into the community. It is equally true
that the community is moving into the libraries and other Directorate
buildings. The cost of upkeep of buildings is extremely high. It
does not make sense if they are not fully used. The neighbourhood
libraries are being gradually adapted to allow space for community
activities and meetings, including events we organize. Pre-school
playgroups, for example, meet in two of our library buildings. Many
libraries have been used for meetings after they close in the evenings,
and this is being extended to day-time meetings too. One of the
great things about West Norwood Library and Nettlefold Hall is
that Nettlefold Hall, complete with refreshments room and bar,
is not only used for meetings, for concerts, talks and films arranged
weekly by LARA, and local drama festivals, it can be hired for
dances and wedding receptions too. Essentially it is a community
building, used by many groups in the community. Are there
problems in adopting this kind of attitude? Yes, of course there are.
The letting of libraries and other buildings in the Directorate involves continual problems—but then the only way to have a trouble-
free life is to do nothing.

Libraries should be live, active, busy places. They are ideal sites
for organized happenings. Why not have poetry readings, folk-jazz
groups, informal visits by authors, theatre workshops? All these
have been tried and worked well. So far most of these activities
have taken place predominantly at West Norwood which is an
ideally spacious and open building. Locally based young actors,
the Incubus Group, run workshops for children there every holiday,

held in the central courtyard of the complex when the weather is fine. The children's library in the Central Zone library in Brixton is as small and inadequate as the rest of that building. However, one Saturday recently many children turned up there to hear Gloria Cameron and members of the Caribbean Drama and Folk Group sing Jamaican folk-songs and tell stories in Jamaican dialect. Several of the neighbourhood libraries are arranging regular afternoon sessions for mothers and babies to meet informally each week with a different speaker. There is infinite scope for all kinds of events like this.

One of our libraries, South Island Library, was closed when the Central Zone changed to the comprehensive/neighbourhood scheme. It is a large building, and had always been under-used. It became uneconomic to keep it open, and as almost everyone in its catchment area was within half a mile of another service point, it was decided to close it as a library. The children's library, a vast room, had taken up the whole of the first floor. Most of the children who came into the library wanted desperately to be entertained, and for someone to pay attention to them. Most of them were flat-dwellers, and the sheer size of the room, combined with the multi-coloured floor tiles proved an irresistible running and jumping ground. Exuberant high spirits and intense frustration were also expressed by breaking windows, and setting off fire-extinguishers. Sometimes children looked at books and even borrowed them, although most of them found reading difficult. Their main problem was to be entertained, and staff who worked there spent a great deal of time just chatting to them.

When the library was closed, it was decided to use the top floor for organized activities for children, and for meetings. Rosalind Clark, who had run a successful workshop for children in Edinburgh for five years, had just moved to London, and Kaye Webb of Puffin Books had discussed with her the possibility of starting a workshop involving members of the Puffin Club. They had no suitable premises. However, Kaye Webb knew of our plans to make full use of buildings. In April 1971 the first session of the South Island Workshop, a joint Lambeth/Puffin Club venture was held, starting with a generous grant from the Puffin Club, and also money from other sources. We had helped to publicise the workshop locally through our contacts, and the majority of the two hundred children who turned up to the first session were local children. It was a great success. Ros Clark had gathered a dazzling group of actors (including some of the Freehold Company from Edinburgh), musicians, poets, and artists to work with the children. Everywhere throughout the former library children were making masks, doing acrobatics, improvizations, making tape-recordings or playing weird musical instruments. It was good to see. The workshop has had many teething troubles, but now it is firmly established and flourishing. Most of the Puffin Club children have dropped out, because they had to travel long distances to get there, and the workshop has gradually become a local affair. Genevieve Draper, who had worked with Rosalind Clark in Edinburgh, took over from her, and the workshop now runs sessions on Saturday afternoons, and also two evenings each week, for children ages five to twelve. Activities include puppetry, drama, painting, clay modelling, acrobatics, mask-making, improvised music and film making. They also have a football team. Local parents are involved on the committee that runs the workshop, as is one of the librarians working with children in that zone, and they meet regularly to plan activities and fund-raising events like jumble sales, also held in the former library. It goes without saying that there are some books lying around in kinderboxes at the workshop. What was unsuccessful just as a library, has become successful as an arts workshop. The building serves children more effectively than it did as a library, although we do plan to extend the use of books there in co-operation with the workshop.

About two miles away from South Island Workshop, a breakaway group of young artists and art teachers, deserters from the Young Friends of the Tate Gallery, run the Pear Place Club. They also meet in one of our ex-libraries (from which we had to move to a temporary building down the road, because the old building was to be pulled down imminently as part of a new scheme in the area— several years later, it still hasn't happened). They run an arts and crafts club for local children, and also take them on outings all over London. Some of the Pear Place group help at South Island

Workshop, and the two groups spark off ideas all the time. In the summer of 1972 they jointly mounted a fascinating exhibition of paintings, claywork, mosaics and models produced by children, which toured various sites in the Directorate. It was tangible evidence of what an extremely enthusiastic, tirelessly hard-working and very talented group of young men and women with creative ideas can draw out of the children they work with.

Here, too, is the evidence, if it is still needed, that librarians should not dabble in puppetry, handicrafts or running children's clubs, for which they have had no training. They can, however, give support and encouragement to those people who *are* specifically trained in such activities, thus being involved as sponsors or initiators rather than as participants.

For the librarian who is community-minded, there are no limits to the possibilities for working through the community both inside and outside the confines of library buildings.

# 4
# Introducing and Publicising Books

British librarians are rather haphazard in the techniques used to introduce books and other materials to people. Our skills in tracing and collating materials are certainly much more highly developed than our techniques of advice to readers. The latter is almost invariably seen as a passive activity. Walk into the average public lending library, and if you want help in selecting a book, you will probably have to take the initiative and approach the librarian yourself. Our colleagues in the United States tend to be much more extrovert about this, and to see reader's advice as a skill which can be taught, and not left to the general assumption that provided you have awareness of the library resources and a reasonably pleasant personality, there is nothing more to be said. Not all librarians are automatically sensitive to people, particularly when they are in-experienced, and I think much more thought and discussion should be given to this subject than appears in our professional press or in accounts of meetings. Maybe we should be more extrovert; however, the librarian who pounces on every reader with the determination shown by many shop assistants towards people who are just looking around would possibly be more disastrous than the self-effacing librarian who has to be sought out by the readers. Our haphazard approach has not helped our image. Nothing unfortunately is more true than that librarians generally, and I am afraid deservedly, have a bad reputation for relations with the public. Take any random group of articulate, educated people. Ask them about their experience of public libraries. Many of them will come up with accounts of indifference, rudeness, mis-information, or bureaucratic obstruction; many will admit to having been intimidated by the reception they have met. If such is their experience, can we wonder that library users are almost exclusively middle-class? Unpalatable though it is, the fact remains: libraries are seen by a large proportion of the population as part of the Establishment. Too often, if they do venture inside, this impression will be confirmed. But librarians are only human. No one would deny that many members of the public are tiresome in the extreme. Can any one of us who has practised as a librarian say that we have never behaved in a way we were ashamed of afterwards when dealing with the public? Like everyone else we are most vulnerable when tired at the end of a long day, when worried by personal problems, or trying to do more than one job at once.

Part of the answer should lie in more discussion of technique and more training; part in ensuring that librarians do not have to spend too many long stretches at public service points, and also that they are free *just* to talk to people, and are not supposed to be doing something else as well. In many children's libraries the librarian is expected to help children find the books they want, as well as being engaged in counter duties. Is it any wonder that children who need help hesitate before approaching a librarian who looks too busy stamping books to have time for their enquiries? I well remember my days working in some of the huge old Carnegie children's libraries in New York. Open weekdays from 3 p.m.—6 p.m, all counter routines were carried out by clerical staff. The librarian never sat down, indeed, as I recall, there was nowhere to sit, but paced the floor continually, besieged by questions. It was exhausting, and essential to wear comfortable shoes, but it lasted for a reasonably limited length of time, and was certainly effective. It would not of course be so effective for a librarian to pace continually round a small room, which could easily give the impression of being on patrol. However, anyone who works with children will soon find out that more of them will approach you once you come out from the counter, inquiry desk or whatever other effective barricade has been erected. It is also true that it helps to wander around carrying a handful of books in a casual way. Some children need and ask for a great deal of guidance and help; some would like it, but are never likely to ask; some are independent and prefer to be left alone; and others come into the library mainly because they want to chat to a friendly adult, or find a warm refuge, or simply to pass the time. In the course of even a short spell of duty in the library, any conscientious librarian will experience the satisfaction of finding the right book for a specific child, as well as the frustration of trying to help, for example, the football enthusiast with limited reading skills who has already borrowed all the current football annuals. I think this aspect of librarianship—the direct and specific advice of a librarian to a child about individual books he or she might enjoy—is extremely important. It is more nebulous than advice about which books will provide information needed for homework, school projects and so on. Its effectiveness is impossible to assess. However, not surprisingly, I think librarians tend to exaggerate the direct influence they exert over children's reading tastes in this way. The school librarian, as already stated, is in an easier position here. It is possible to get to know many children quite well within the school framework, and reading guidance of a direct, personal kind can follow a more organized and regular pattern. Contact with the public library is bound to be more spasmodic. The child in the school library is only with his peers. In the public library, some will be with their parents, others with siblings or friends, or alone. The librarian must be sensitive to the appropriate reactions. I remember a well-meaning colleague, friendly and maternal, who once told me 'I never let children go out of the library without having a word with them, to make sure they have found what they want'. What a nightmare her library must have been for the self-contained child! She had forgotten a very important fact which librarians should never overlook. Reading is essentially a private, personal activity, and in our anxiety to make sure children are finding what they want, we should not intrude on their privacy. Obviously librarians have an innate curiosity about children's reading tastes, but this should be kept in check. Is it surprising for example, that children so often borrow books on sex without having them checked out, and then return them surreptitiously to the shelves? I can see valid reasons why some school librarians keep records of books read by individual children, but I can't help finding it distasteful.

Many parents too run the risk of killing their children's interest in reading by over-anxiety or insensitive interference. Two such I remember vividly from the days when I worked in a children's library. One, a devoted father, worked locally, but lived in Kent. He regularly borrowed books for his daughter, who turned out to be twelve. When he consulted me about her reading, I suggested that she would find it more satisfactory to choose her own books. 'Oh, no,' he replied. 'You see, I read every book before she does, so that I can discuss it with her afterwards'. The other was a mother who used to follow her pale, hag-ridden son of about ten round the library shelves every Saturday, determined he should read *good* books. One day, after a prolonged argument at the other side of the room, she dragged him over to the counter, and said to me 'Now, wouldn't he like *Peter Pan*?' She was naturally furious when I told her that I didn't see any reason why he should. Often conscientious parents with limited education themselves tend to press their children into reading the *classics*, because they think it will be good for them; meanwhile trendy parents encourage three year olds to develop their independence by selecting their own books, clearly believing that what matters most is for them not to be thwarted in the right to make their own choices. Both attitudes can be disastrous, and sometimes a librarian can help when such incidents happen in the library. Certainly the opportunity often occurs for chatting to parents casually about children's reading, and this can be as important as talking to children. However, it should be a sobering thought that the most popular books are those children recommend to each other. This is hardly surprising. They are only doing what adults do—passing on information to each other about books they have enjoyed. It is intriguing to think of books as diverse as *Stig of the Dump* and *Charlie and the Chocolate Factory* which achieved tremendous popularity without any prompting from adults, long before the former was televised or the latter filmed. I think it is important for librarians to try to introduce books to individual children in the library, but we should always have a sense of proportion about how much success we are likely to have.

Certainly we should try to draw children's attention to books in a variety of ways, although here too, we should be quite clear what we are doing. Books and reading can be pushed in ways which are highly dubious. I have no time whatsoever for any of the variations on the old-fashioned idea of the *story tree*, which is nowadays often called a *summer reading programme*, in which children are given reading lists of *good* books to race through, in order to add a leaf to a tree or a star to a sky each time they can prove they have read one. Defenders of the system claim that at least the children taking part will have read a number of books. My contention is that this is a valueless exercise if they have rushed through them in order to notch up another leaf or star. Reading should be for enjoyment, not to achieve pseudo-goals, and such methods defeat what should be their purpose. I found when I worked in the United States that some teachers encouraged reading by giving homework in the form of an injunction to read a book and write a book report on it. Before I knew about this, I remember being puzzled by the number of children who came into the library ingenuously asking for 'a good, thin book'.

Casual reading-aloud sessions in the library are a good idea, particularly in the holidays, when so many children get bored. I believe this should be done spontaneously as the need arises, and not as an organized programme. It will be very different from the more organized reading which can take place in a school library or a school classroom with a known group of children.

Exhibitions and displays can be an effective way of drawing attention to specific categories of books. However, it is necessary to be quite clear about the purpose, the limits to be imposed, and the audience at whom the exhibition is directed. A successful exhibition must be carefully planned and thought through, as well as being displayed in a sufficiently sophisticated way. People expect to find books in libraries, so that the reasons behind an exhibition must be apparent for it to have any impact at all. As modern eyes are satiated by advertising, an exhibition has to be eye-catching, but there is no point making an effort to attract attention if a display has no apparent objective. It was still possible to get away with fairly mindless exhibitions in the mid-to-late fifties, when a laminated book jacket in itself constituted a refreshing and pleasing sight. This is no longer true. As far as the modern child is concerned, it is just one of the facts of life that library books have laminated jackets. There are so many books published that it is not very helpful to mount large comprehensive exhibitions—the result can be as bewildering to the outsider as the library shelves.

It should go without saying that exhibitions for children should normally include use of music, slides, films, illustrative materials and anything else relevant to the subject. How to choose a subject? One factor to take into account is the size of the display area. *World Exploration* is clearly unsuitable for a small library, whereas *Freshwater Fishes* would be appropriate. Sadly, the most limiting factor is usually not the building, but the children's books. Most reasonably modern ideas are out, just because there are so few books for children about contemporary life, whatever the subject under consideration. Naturally relevant adult books should be included, but it does not make sense if they form the major proportion of an exhibition aimed mainly at ages up to twelve. It should be fun to do an exhibition on the year 2,000, which is, after all, not far away; or on such a currently fashionable topic as pollution; however, neither subject is bibliographically feasible if books are to be included in the display. Subjects like air travel or ballet are naturals for a children's exhibition. No need to create the interest, and attractive displays are easy to arrange. But which of us wants to draw attention to dreary series books on how an aeroplane works, how an airport functions, how a pilot trains, or dimly illustrated ballet anthologies including only the most traditional companies and dancers in the most well-worn classical ballets as performed about six years ago? It is understandable to react by choosing a comprehensive subject like *The Sea*, in order to include deep sea fishes, the Royal National Lifeboat Association, and Sir Francis Drake—but the result would be muddle and confusion.

In Lambeth there has been a long tradition of Book Festivals (formerly Book Weeks) which began in the early 1950's, and followed the same general pattern, though with increasing sophistication, from 1957 until 1972, which marked the beginning of a change in emphasis. Staff at each library chose a theme for an exhibition of books and related materials designed to highlight some aspect of the bookstock, in conjunction with a display that would transform each library for a fortnight. It was an attempt to pinpoint and focus the library services to children at each individual service point, and as it was locally based, to give staff at each library scope to carry out their own ideas within the framework of the Festival. The actual fortnight, latterly in May although other times were tried too, was always a time of frenzy and heightened activity, with organized parties from local schools visiting the exhibition and also attending talks on the theme of the exhibition, and meeting authors and artists. The Festival always took nine months to plan. Each September libraries were issued with an aide-memoire pad, giving details of all information required by the Children's Librarian, Music Librarian, Graphic Designer, Central Administration and the Foreman Porter, and the dates when such information was required. Everything relating to the Festival was included, ranging from the title of the exhibition, names and credentials of subject speakers, requirements for audio-visual equipment, taped music, additional display equipment, lists of exhibits to be borrowed from outside organizations, and forms for speakers to sign on the day of their talks. Suggested themes were discussed with the Assistant Director and the Children's Librarian before being approved, and planning and discussion continued throughout the nine months period. General publicity was designed by the Graphic Designer, who also advised about methods of display, although obviously not able to mount displays at the thirteen service points. The Festival was always co-ordinated by the Children's Librarian. Our aim, never fully realized, had been to present an enjoyable and well-thought-out Festival expressing unity in diversity.

A successful exhibition depends on working out clearly the extent and limits of the chosen theme, as well as the approach to the subject. As I mentioned earlier, a theme like *The Sea* could easily result in a diffused and utterly meaningless display, unless it is decided to concentrate on one issue, like ships, or underwater life. There is a marked tendency, we have found, for staff to prefer a historical approach—not surprising, in view of the bibliography of most subjects, but it can become tedious. The favourite angle is to chose a theme like *From Papyrus to the Modern Book* or *From Leonardo da Vinci to Concorde*, so that a great range of books and exhibits can be thrown in. We have tried in recent years to encourage participatory exhibitions, rather than displays where *everything* is under glass, and the atmosphere not unlike that of an old-fashioned museum. This is not easy to achieve. Some exhibitions have gone too far in the zeal

for participation, and libraries have been filled with children
frenziedly pushing buttons on working models until they broke
down, to the exclusion of all else; on the other hand a fairly recent
exhibition *Rhythm and Music* proved a tremendously effective
choice, the whole library enlivened by festive music, and by children
trying out improvised musical instruments, as well as groups making
music with more orthodox instruments. Some displays have been
explicit and self-explanatory; the complexity of others has required
a guided tour; some have been didactic, and seized on by teachers
for instant projects; others have cleverly managed to convey something of the pleasure and enjoyment to be experienced in art or
music. It is not only necessary to plan the layout of the exhibits in a
coherent pattern, allowing for the idiosyncrasies of each building,
but also to integrate the books properly into the display, which is
psychologically as well as graphically most important. A library
with a very spacious children's room once chose the theme *Ships and
Shipping*. Fascinating models from the National Maritime Museum
and the Port of London Authority were displayed in rather solid
cases round which children crowded; meanwhile, at the far end of
the room was a book display, almost totally ignored, and bearing no
apparent relation to the exhibits. Sometimes staff have encouraged
the participation of schools in creating displays. I have always been
strongly opposed to this. The result inevitably looks like a primary
school classroom rather than a professional display. It involves
participation for the small number of children who contributed
to the display, but must be very disappointing for all the others. It is
a fallacy that children enjoy looking at work done by other children.
There is no reason why libraries shouldn't sometimes have displays
of paintings and other work done at school by children, but Book
Festival has never seemed the right occasion for this. One year one
of our libraries chose the theme *Let's go Fishing* and the display
included fishing rods, tackle and other accessories friezes round the
wall and fish mobiles made by local children. It would have been far
more effective to mount a display showing how to make your own
fishing equipment in easy stages; linked with maps showing the
best places to fish in London; and clear identification charts showing
the type of fish to be found in each area.

The help of outside organizations in contributing to our Festivals has been overwhelming. I well remember the mild surprise of the then Curator of the Horniman Museum when I first approached him years ago with a request to borrow a stuffed golden eagle for one of our early exhibitions. He had never had such a request from a library before, but was most helpful. Since that time hardly a year has passed when the Horniman Museum has not lent us exhibits ranging from shells, fossils, and musical instruments to Samurai armour and swords. Most of the large museums in London have been approached from time to time, and many of them have been extremely helpful. A recent find was the Wellcome Institute of the History of Medicine which proved extremely generous in lending exhibits from their horrendous collection of early medical instruments, which naturally proved a great attraction. Commercial organizations have often seen the Festival as an opportunity for publicity, and have been extremely helpful, and sometimes willing to mount their own displays. Harrods zoo department one year lent live animals, although my own view was that the attendant problems vastly outweighed the advantages of such live exhibits. We have always tried to involve local organizations, groups and individuals in the Festival. Fortunately for us, the administrative headquarters of the National Theatre Company is in Lambeth, and just as they have always used their nearest library for information needs of all kinds, so they have been generous in helping us. As a life-long theatre addict, I still remember with awe a Sunday morning some years ago, spent watching as the Head of Costume for the Company and Laurence Olivier's dresser arranged costumes, swords and armour in display cases for an exhibition due to start the next day. Also in the borough is the Oval, and the Surrey County Cricket Club have been helpful in contributing to displays of quite a different kind. Innumerable local people with special skills, as well as a wide variety of organizations, have helped us too.

It has taken years, and much bitter experience, to try and foresee all the problems and crises that will arise when organizing an event on this scale. One which should have been foreseen happened years ago at our Carnegie Library, which is a solid building, typical of its kind. Part of an exhibition there on *Prehistoric Life* was to be a collection of fossils from the Science Museum, which was delivered ensconced in one of those huge old-fashioned plate glass display cases. The librarian had checked the dimensions of the case, and ascertained that it would go through the door into the children's library. What he hadn't checked was that it was too wide for the main front door, and that six men were needed to lift it. The case was deposited on the pavement while an urgent call went out for six men to help lift it through a side door. Once one of our librarians persuaded the British Museum to lend us two priceless Greek vases for his display about Greek myths. They were lent on condition that we arranged for them to be professionally packed and transported, insured them very heavily, and provided a twenty-four hour guard. The vases naturally looked superb, but the cost both in terms of money and strain on the staff was too great. The porter allocated to the night watch found the building uncomfortably eerie, and took his dog for company. Several of us had sleepless nights until the vases were safely back in the museum. This was a case of being too ambitious. Another year, the live animals previously mentioned proved predictably popular with visitors, but this led to a very unnecessary incident when we had a speaker talking to a group of children. At the back of the room, behind the audience, were the animals, including a monkey. As the speaker began, the vile monkey found a tin spoon in its cage, and began beating loudly on the metal bars to attract attention. It took several minutes to get the key to the cage and remove the spoon. It was the kind of incident we should have been able to avoid.

In recent years the most effective exhibitions, which have demonstrated unity of theme and execution, are easy to recall. Most of them have been based on a simple idea. One was *The Painter's World*. The idea was to mount a display of large reproductions of famous paintings (in an area where few children would be likely to have visited an art gallery); to emphasize the different techniques in art by linking brushes, paintboxes, pastels, crayons and oils with pictures created by these different techniques, and also to give clear explanatory notes on each technique. Reproductions of paintings came from several sources, including the Arts Council and the Lambeth Council collection, which is scattered in libraries and

Council buildings throughout the borough. Considerable ingenuity was required in tracking down all the best paintings, and arranging for substitutes to be put up when they were borrowed from key sites in the Town Hall. As well as the how-to-do-it books on show, which tend to be serviceable and rather pedestrian, there was a magnificent range of expensive adult art books. Most children who came to the exhibition would never have seen, let alone handled such beautiful books.

*Exploring Space* was a popular choice in 1968, when space travel still captured the public imagination. Kodak lent a magnificent display of breathtakingly beautiful colour photographs; the U.S. Information Service and the Embassy of the U.S.S.R. also lent photographic material relating to their space programmes; the G.P.O. provided a working model of a satellite station, plus models of Telstar and Early Bird. There was a comprehensive display of science fiction added to the necessarily small collection of those factual books on the subject which had not dated. This was not an exhibition *just* for children. People of all ages thronged round the Kodak photographs, and also turned up for showings of the Russian film *Walk In Space*.

*The Book of the Film* juxtaposed stills from films with the books from which they had originated. The library was blacked out, and visitors walked into a large room lit only by spotlights picking out the film stills, the books, posters, and the main exhibit, a film camera and editing equipment. The retrospective reflections of one of the staff who arranged the exhibition are interesting:

The arrangement lent itself very well to conducted class tours, allowing fair flexibility according to age group, although the under-sevens were perhaps rather left out. . . . The film-making equipment was explained to each class at the appropriate level. The response varied from good to excellent, with several surprises, such as the group of eight-year olds who drained us of every morsel of technical detail we possessed as they scrambled over the equipment, and the usually intensely cynical group of girls from a local secondary school, who were tamed the moment they glimpsed the poster of Steve McQueen.

These comments pinpoint two important facts. One is that it is hardly ever possible to choose a theme which will appeal to every age-group, and it is probably best not to try. We have found in

recent years that groups ranging from pre-school playgroups to the
lower forms of secondary schools have been willing to come on
group visits to exhibitions if they are suitable. My own feeling has
always been that it does not matter, as long as the same library does
not mount an exhibition two years running which has an appeal to
the same limited age group. It would be foolish not to aim predominantly at 7–11 years-olds, as most primary schools are keen to
send their children on group visits; but the theme can extend either
upwards or downwards from that level. The other fact is that the
staff need to spend time and care in reading up the background of
their chosen subject, so that they can explain the exhibits in an
interesting way, and also answer questions. Some exhibitions are
more explanatory than others; but staff should be able to make all of
them come more alive when showing groups around.

   *Playing with Junk* proved a most imaginative exhibition. It was
mainly the inspiration of an art student from the City and Guilds of
London Art School, who worked with the staff to completely transform the library. The visitor entering the hallway was greeted by a
series of superb enlarged photographs of art created from junk,
interspersed with pictures of piles of old junk photographed locally
by two of the staff. In the children's library were strange creatures
made from junk including a huge black and white spotted cow with
an attendant milkmaid on wheels (who was pushed around the
library continually, and had to be repaired about every two days);
a weird contraption based on a laundry basket, with handles and
wheels to turn; a magnificent and massive creature created out of
tins; a city of boxes which children could crawl inside; endless
mobiles, and a huge collage dominating one end of the room, which
viewed from one angle was a dinosaur, from another a rocket. In
amongst the exhibits were the books, suggesting further ideas for
junk modelling. Children naturally revelled in this exhibition, and it
was a delight to see them pulling, pushing and experimenting with
the models. There was only one dissident, an old lady heard mutter-
ing to herself as she left the building 'Never seen such a lot of old
junk—I can't think what the place is coming to'.

   Two exhibitions in 1971 provided a dramatic contrast. At one
library, *Art, Literature and Music of the Caribbean* generated great

local enthusiasm. Paintings and sculptures loaned by Caribbean artists living in Britain formed a background, together with the books, for a programme of activities. Over a hundred children turned up one evening for a concert of West Indian folksongs and dancing, given by a local group; Nadia Catouse, the folk-singer held a large audience entranced as she talked and sang; a girl from a local secondary school came to read her own poetry aloud; and Andrew Salkey spent a whole Saturday morning talking about the literature of the Caribbean with sixth form boys from a school round the corner. This was a very successful series of happenings held against a colourful background display.

The comprehensive/neighbourhood experiment started in Central Zone in 1970, and in the next year the staff decided to combine resources and work on the most ambitious and well-thought out exhibition ever mounted during a Book Festival. The theme was complex: *Science and Belief*—a chronicle of man's development within his environment, with special emphasis on the conflict between science and superstition. The main exhibition was staged in the Town Hall, with supporting displays in the libraries. It was divided into four main stages: the Classical Greek/Roman Age; the Renaissance; the 18th/19th Centuries; the 21st Century. The aim was to show how in each period, scientific advance has been in conflict with superstition and ignorance. The Renaissance section for example contrasted astronomy and astrology; medicine and traditional cures; the way in which travel and discovery opened up a wider environment at the same time destroying previously held beliefs. The exhibits in this section included early navigational instruments and medical research equipment, together with symbols of deep-rooted suspicions, like a cow-unbewitcher—a wooden spoon with a hole in the middle, which was placed over a bewitched cow's udder before milking, a process guaranteed to unbewitch any cow. The exhibition had a wide age appeal, and operated at many levels. It could only have been achieved by a group of specialists. Librarians carried out the necessary research, visited museums and other organizations to look at appropriate exhibits to borrow; chose photographs to be blown up; planned the sequence and wrote the excellent captions which clearly guided the exhibition, as well as selecting the books; the Graphic Designers planned the layout and supervised the setting up of the exhibition; the lighting was professionally done; and the Music Librarian worked closely with the team and recorded suitable music, some of which he composed himself, to accompany each section of the display. The result was a highly professional, sophisticated and intelligent exhibition. However, all the staff admitted in retrospect that a project on this scale should have been planned for at least two years in advance. The cost to them was almost total exhaustion before the exhibition had even begun.

These two exhibitions pinpoint many of the problems which have beset Book Festivals over the years. In one, events took place against a background display; in the other energies were concentrated on an extremely complex exhibition. Because the Festival has always been a time for *events* as well as an exhibition, it has tended to be a period of near-frenzy. Although each time there have been some which are excellent, there have also been some very much below the standard we hoped to achieve. Too many of them have shown little evidence of real thought in the planning stages, or the displays have not been managed with sufficient skill or sophistication. Very often staff have worked hard, but the end result has not shown this. People tend to choose complicated themes, and make things more difficult for themselves than they need be.

We have decided that in future the two elements of the Festival, an exhibition and events connected with it, will be separated. The Festival will inevitably take a different form, as it will in future be based on each zone, rather than on individual libraries, and a team of staff in each area will be able to work together on ideas. It may well be that it will seem best to stage the Festival in different zones at different times in the year. And exhibitions can be planned for buildings within the Directorate other than libraries. What better site for a big exhibition than a pool? Also, I hope we shall be able to get away from the idea of a *Children's* Book Festival—so many of the exhibitions have had a limitless appeal, and the themes have often been taken up in allied displays of adult books. Several times in recent years, the same theme has been tackled from different angles appropriate to different age groups in the community, and this idea has infinite possibilities. As with almost everything we do, I have often been asked 'Do Book Festivals have any *value*? Can you see any tangible *results* after having them in Lambeth for so many years?' When people ask about *results* in this way, they usually mean only to ask do Festivals lead to more registered readers, and more books issued? The answer is probably no. But then such a question should be irrelevant. I believe exhibitions are extremely valuable when they are exciting, imaginative and well-organized. A bad exhibition is counter-productive. Anything which draws attention to books and relates them to other aspects of life is valuable; anything which makes libraries into lively, vivid and contemporary places is good; it is my hope that children growing up in Lambeth may think of libraries as places where they have seen interesting exhibitions rather than as storehouses for books. Why don't more libraries mount exhibitions and Festivals? Still comparatively few of them do. They need thought, planning and organization. They need not involve spending vast amounts of money. With very few exceptions we have found that everyone we have approached with a view to borrowing exhibits has been most co-operative and interested.

We have decided to separate events from the Festival, because there is no reason why they should be linked in this way. Events like visits of authors and artists require careful preparation, and we have come to believe that it will work much better to concentrate and plan for one event at a time. Each zone aims to arrange one event for children each month, which may be anything from an author visit to a theatre workshop or a concert. When I first used to invite authors to Lambeth, they were asked to come and talk to groups of children from local schools. After the talk, they answered questions. As time went on, it became obvious that this was not the best method. There is no reason to suppose that people who write or illustrate children's books are also good at public speaking—or indeed at meeting children at all. If they are, it is a bonus. We should never forget that the main energies of creative writers and artists go into creating books. Sometimes a writer or artist who is particularly good with children is harassed by requests to visit libraries, and this is most unfair. My own experience is that it is always best to talk to the publisher first before inviting authors. Sometimes a writer whose books are popular and approachable turns out to be a taciturn and shy person, who should not be subjected to a group of children. Equally there are some writers to whom children should not be subjected. I remember one such, many years ago, who was extremely irritable, and snapped at an enthusiastic ten-year-old, who quite reasonably asked her a fairly innocuous and easily side-tracked personal question. The poor child was understandably upset, and I never asked that writer to Lambeth again. However, such people are in the minority. In recent years, writers and artists have been invited to Lambeth to meet groups of children informally, rather than to give talks. This has to be carefully planned. It is a waste of time to invite groups of children to meet a writer if they haven't read any of the writer's books. It is also supremely discourteous to the writer. We have tended to rely mainly on inviting groups from local schools, ensuring that they have had sets of the appropriate books for weeks before the visit, and that they will have been prepared for this either by the teacher, or by one of our staff visiting the school. In many cases this has worked extremely well, and the most dedicated and involved teachers have taken time and care to prepare for the occasion. I think it would be interesting to develop the idea by inviting a writer to meet a random group of children on a Saturday or during the holidays. The preparation for this could go on for several months beforehand, with displays, talks and readings from the writer's books at different places in the Directorate, leading up to the visit. Fraught with problems, it would still be fun to try. What is the value of such meetings? It is as intangible as the value of Book Festivals. I think it does matter that children should sometimes have the chance to see the writer behind the book, and the artist behind the illustration. It helps to emphasize not only that books are created by real people, but also that the best ones are not *easily* created; quite apart from the pleasure of meeting an interesting and interested person. Many of the writers and illustrators who have been to Lambeth have made a great impression on the children who have met them, and it is true that it generates interest in their books too. I feel I have been very privileged to meet so many of them over the years on such enjoyable occasions in Lambeth, and I have very much appreciated how seriously all of them have taken their meetings with children. One thing I feel very strongly. Librarians who invite writers and artists to meet children are under an obligation not only to see that everything down to the last detail is highly organized; but also that their visitors are courteously received and entertained. A librarian who works for an authority too mean to offer a reasonable fee, travelling expenses and a meal to visitors, should never invite anyone. My comments may sound harsh, but I have heard so many hair-raising stories of visitors being cursorily treated or inadequately paid.

Exhibitions of children's books aimed at adults can be extremely valuable. I know exactly why our annual *First Seven Years* exhibition of books for young children is so successful. It is a simple theme, and limited in scope. There are usually about one hundred and fifty titles included; they have been carefully selected, and represent the considered viewpoint of a group of librarians; adult interest in books for young children does not have to be forced—it is already there, and merely needs a focus; picture books are decorative and eye-catching, and there are usually a fair number included, as well as original illustrations lent by publishers. Once the books have been selected and bought, and copy for the simple checklist prepared, the rest is left to our graphic designers, who invariably interpret our ideas in the most imaginative and creative way. An exhibition of this kind can be left to speak for itself; on the other hand, when it is on tour in health centres, community centres and similar places, it gives staff a reason for spending time there for the odd half hour at busy periods. When we tried this the first time the exhibition toured in 1972, we found it was not easy. Young mothers at health centres with their babies were often understandably pre-occupied, or thought their children were too young, and that the exhibition was not relevant to them; or they were hesitant to approach the book display, an unfamiliar sight in that setting. Staff had to work hard to try and interest them, and more often than not they ended up talking about anything but books. One librarian who was on duty at a centre near the block of flats where she lived found the easiest point of contact was to discuss the drawbacks and advantages of the flats with the mothers, most of whom lived in similar blocks. Some of the staff were worried because it had seemed perhaps a waste of time, and they had not managed to talk about books. However, I don't think that mattered. At least they were making the point that libraries care about getting books to children, and also proving that librarians are human. More and more, I think all of us realize how inexperienced we are in such situations, and how little we know about how to handle them. Most of us feel shy on many occasions when embarking on a new venture. All of us need to be both sensitive and humble when faced with encounters with people, particularly those unfamiliar with books or libraries, and to realize how inexperienced we are, and that we are sure to make mistakes. Ultimately what matters most, possibly making a fool of oneself, or finding out more about the local community and how best to serve it?

When the exhibition was parked for a week in a double-decker bus outside Waterloo Station, the situation provided a different kind of challenge. Unfortunately the week we had chosen to take this site at the busiest of all London's mainline stations coincided with a 'go-slow' on British Rail, and the commuters we had hoped to attract tended understandably to be more involved with catching trains or getting into the office after an unbearably long journey than with looking at children's books. In spite of this, the exhibition attracted a number of visitors, and a fair amount of comment. Some people were surprised that we should be doing such a thing; others clearly wondered what the catch was, and were hesitant to commit themselves by coming inside; yet others were genuinely seeking information about their children's reading. We found that many people looked firmly the other way, having noticed a stationary bus filled with books and painted white instead of the traditional red; some approached warily, and began to read the poster outside. We learnt that if at that point we either emerged on to the platform of the bus, or looked eagerly out of the window and caught their eyes as they looked up, we had probably lost them. If on the other hand we took no notice, and studiously looked at books, some of them would venture inside. If there were a couple of people already inside the bus, others quickly followed. We decided another time it might almost be worthwhile to pay a couple of stooges to pose continually as interested members of the public looking at books, just to get the others in! This particular experiment

*Above:* Book exhibition at a community centre

*Below:* Storytelling by the pool

Storytelling in the park

also pointed up the advantages of our system in which all librarians are expected to carry out any professional duties. The exhibition was open daily, including Saturday and Sunday, from 8 a.m. to 6.30 p.m. for a whole week, and staff were on duty for two and a half hour shifts. It would have been extremely difficult to cover all these times involving only staff working with children, and some of their other regular commitments might have had to be cancelled. As it was, we did not manage to fit in every librarian who offered to do a shift. Briefing sessions, including a short introductory talk on the books to be displayed, were held beforehand, and staff spent some amount of time looking at the books. Queries which could not be answered on the spot by staff on duty on the bus were written down, and sent daily to the Children's Librarian's office. Replies were then sent by post. Understandably, some of the queries could have been answered on the spot by staff more familiar with children's books; but that did not matter, as long as they were answered in the end. Undoubtedly many of the staff working mainly with adults were also asked questions about adult books which they were able to answer on the spot.

The area of Lambeth around Waterloo Station is crammed with office blocks ranging from the Department of Education and Science, and the Central Office of Information to Shell, Petrofina, and County Hall, headquarters of the Greater London Council (GLC). All were visited beforehand, and asked to display our posters. The different reactions were extremely amusing. One government department was not impressed by our suggestion that the poster was extremely relevant to their staff, as presumably a fair proportion of them had children under seven, and an official nervously showed us the door, explaining on the way out of their bare and monolithic building that there was actually no *space* for posters! Sometimes we were treated with the faint distaste usually reserved for door-to-door salesmen; however, many other firms were extremely co-operative, interested and helpful. The possibilities for developing this kind of exhibition are boundless. Most people have children, and many of them can be interested in anything which relates to their children, provided it is competently and confidently presented, and is also easily accessible.

I don't believe that interest in children's books either is or should be confined to books which are currently available here. Britain is not the world. Children's books from other countries are often extremely interesting. In Lambeth we have held exhibitions of children's books from the German Democratic Republic and from Poland. Both exhibitions happened because of contacts I had made when I was invited to join a group of people working with children in art, the theatre and books, on a two-week visit to Moscow and Leningrad. Once you start, such things are comparatively easy to organize, and people are very keen to co-operate. I was later able to arrange for the first exhibition of English children's books to be held in the German Democratic Republic at the State Library in East Berlin. I was responsible for selecting the books, and the Book Development Council made all the arrangements.

There are always many opportunities for librarians to talk to parents or groups of adults working with children about books. There is no doubt about the fact that there is an intense and often latent interest in children's books amongst many parents. The rapid development of Books for Children Groups throughout the country, as well as the energy and imagination so many of them devote to varied activities, is proof enough, apart from anything else. Librarians should seize every opportunity to stimulate this interest by giving talks to large or small groups of parents, and by publicizing this activity as much as possible. If a librarian demonstrates a willingness to speak word soon gets around, and more invitations will follow. Here again, librarians must be flexible in their attitudes, and prepared to plunge into any situation. Inevitably some audiences will turn out to be articulate, argumentative and hard to convince; others will be receptive and extremely responsive. It is sad but true, that often those who are theoretically well-educated turn out to be rather arrogant and less willing to admit that they might have something to learn about children's books!

I am sure too that many of us have not begun to explore the possibilities of talking about books to children. I have already commented on my views on this in a library situation. I should like to try and develop ideas for doing this in a less formal way in other places. It will not be easy, and I cannot pretend to have formulated my ideas about this very clearly yet. I can envisage staff wandering into play areas and sports centres with a handful of books, sitting down to chat about them, perhaps reading aloud from one of them; it could be utterly disastrous—but I have a feeling it could work at least sometimes if we find the right approach.

I think most of us don't yet exploit enough the links we could have with children's books which are televised or filmed. We tend to stop short at stocking up on extra copies of books which are already read when they are shown on television; it is a broad generalization that a book which is a shelf-sticker will not be helped by being televised, although those which are moderately popular can be boosted in this way. In Lambeth we haven't got much further than a rather disastrous experiment years ago to show the *Jackanory* programme in a library each afternoon. We hoped naïvely that this might lead to a situation in which we could chat about the stories being told afterwards. Unfortunately, at the time *Jackanory* was going through a particularly bad patch, and the stories told the first week could best be described as boring. Instead of gathering perceptive comments which we had hoped to feed back to the *Jackanory* producers, the only ones we had were crude in the extreme and accompanied by insistent demands to switch to the other channel! It was our fault—the idea was a non-starter. Why should children, who might well sometimes watch the programme reasonably quietly at home come round the corner to the library just to do so?

We have found the Weston Woods films of picture books extremely useful with young children. We have used their filmstrips (which we always laboriously turned into slides, which are so much more practical because they are easier to handle) intermittently for some years, but have more or less switched over to the films now, as they are generally more effective. The only problem is that there are so few of them available. We have run programmes during the school holidays touring to day nurseries, health centres, One O'Clock Clubs and similar places, taking multiple copies of the books with us too. Very often this has led to opportunities for sitting on the floor afterwards with the children, talking with them as they look at the books. Young children are usually very excited as well as puzzled to find in a book the pictures they have just seen on film. Particularly in the day nurseries, where the same group of children are likely to be there in a controlled situation, the staff have found it very helpful to keep the books and read and look at them with the children over the next few weeks after films are shown. This is only a beginning. As libraries develop their use of media other than books, so will the opportunities for this kind of activity increase. At the moment despite the proliferation of audio-visual aids, *good* material relating directly to children's books is extremely scarce. However, this is only one angle we should consider. As far as one knows, not many libraries in this country are yet developing the kind of programmes involving films and other media which are familiar in other countries. In New York Public Library the Young Adult Services Division has generated and sponsored an ambitious programme, with the help of a grant from an outside body, which has enabled young people to make their own experimental films, which have then been shown in library programmes. Librarians have found, not surprisingly, that it is easier to make initial contact with young people through films rather than through books.

Back to books, and to one of the most long-lived ways of introducing books—storytelling. Storytelling has been part of the tradition of children's librarianship from the very early days of the profession. When I first began to work with children, I was utterly opposed to it, because most discussions on the subject seemed to me overlaid with sentimentality, and young librarians who were adherents tended to talk about storytelling in such a precious way that I found it impossible to relate the practice they described to the children I knew in Brixton. My year in the United States re-inforced my attitudes, as New York Library followed, and still follows, a rigid and curiously ritualistic pattern of storytelling, but the staff there did also tell stories in summer in Central Park, and it was seeing one of these in action which began radically to change my views about storytelling. Perhaps what was wrong was the setting and not the storytelling? So many libraries had deliberately planned quite excruciating 'story hour rooms'. Storytelling had become isolated as an activity which took place in libraries, and it was often even separated off within the library. Yet traditionally storytelling had

taken place where people happened to be. Wasn't it creating
difficulties anyway to try and collect an audience inside the library?
To put up a notice saying 'Storytelling in the library at 11 a.m. on
Tuesdays' is not likely to produce much response without additional
publicity, and even then may attract only a few children. Meanwhile
there may be a park not five minutes walk away, overflowing with
them. Even an ice-cream van doesn't remain static with a notice
saying 'Ice-cream on sale here'. The driver goes where he knows
children are. And ice-cream is demonstrably more popular than
storytelling. I don't see how even librarians who cling nostalgically
to the idea of storytelling in libraries can fail to see that it must
inevitably be more effective in other places, except at those times
when the library is likely to be full and busy, which is probably when
staff can least be spared anyway.

In Lambeth the holiday storytelling programme we have developed
since 1970 is one of the most vivid and effective ways we have found
of demonstrating our belief that librarians should move out into
the community. From 1966, we had experimented in a small way,
telling stories in three local parks each summer. In 1970 the programme began in earnest, and we visited twenty sites each week. By
1972, we had extended to forty-six sessions each week.

Every weekday during the six week school summer holiday period,
one team goes out each morning, two each afternoon. A team
consists of two storytellers, who travel round by car with a driver,
who is responsible for looking after the public address equipment—
a microphone, amplifier, battery and loud-speaker, also two banners,
and groundsheets for use on damp grass. During the course of a
morning or afternoon, a team generally visits three sites, and stories
are told at each one for about twenty-five minutes. On arrival, for
example, in a park, the car drives up to the selected site (chosen in
co-operation with the Park Superintendent, and at a strategic spot
near where most children play). A tree is always used as a background in parks. One of the canvas banners on a flagpole is set up on
site, and fastened with tent pegs and guy ropes into the ground; the
equipment is set up and tested by one of the storytellers, whilst the
other storyteller carries the other banner shoulder-high round the
park to collect an audience. I know very well that some people find

this hard to do. It is quite possible to walk through a small play-ground asking every passing child if they want to come and listen, and shouting to those frenetically swinging or sliding, only to end up with a very small group. It is necessary to become hardened to getting a negative response, and also to having to walk past rows of adults on park benches, carrying a banner. I have a strong exhibi-tionist streak, and enjoy it immensely, but I have noticed that some people are rather hesitant, and tend to skirt round the edges of a group. I have known a timid person round up an audience of only fifty in a busy park, whereas the next week, in similar conditions, a bolder one could produce a hundred and fifty.

Who are the storytellers? Until 1972 they were all librarians, but certainly not all librarians working with children. We have always invited any interested librarian to apply, because we believe that storytelling is likely to appeal to people with varied skills and interests, and whether they have experience of working with children in the library or not is probably irrelevant. In 1972, when the pro-gramme expanded to forty-six sessions from the twenty-six held in 1971, it was essential to recruit outside people as storytellers. It was decided this should not be on a voluntary basis, but that people engaged should be paid for their services, and that each person we appointed should be asked to come for six sessions during the holiday period. We felt that a librarian should always be one of the two storytellers in each team. We advertised in *The Guardian, New Society* and a lively and radical local paper, asking those interested in taking part in the storytelling programme to ring the Children's Librarian's office. About a hundred and fifty people rang for further details. We then sent them a handout, describing the programme in detail, and deliberately quoting extracts from reports on some of the toughest sessions the previous year. If still interested, they were asked to learn a story, and given alternative dates to choose to come for audition. Predictably, as we had hoped, this put many of them off, and only thirty agreed to come for audition, and some of these failed to show up on the day. Meeting those who came was a fascinating experience. Each one was briefly auditioned, and had an informal interview with us, and also with the Personnel Officer. We had thought it might be difficult to make decisions about which of them to select, but in fact it was quite easy. There were men and women of all ages, ranging from teachers, social workers, actors, to students and housewives. Several of them would clearly not have fitted in with our existing team, but most of them were both interesting and responsive. When it came to the audition, we had a number of surprises. Sometimes sensitive young people started on a story, obviously quite unaware that they were talking down to children. Many of them had chosen stories more suitable for very young children anyway, and this made it much worse. I am usually very impressed by some of the commune-dwelling, sensitive and gentle young men and women who are drawn to work with children in workshops, play areas and various 'alternative' organizations. It was curious to see that several of them who came for audition adopted the most old-fashioned and didactic tone when telling stories. We had asked everyone to choose traditional tales for audition. Many of them didn't, and chose instead rather unremarkable and sentimental stories which were badly written, and impossible to tell. This was the case with more than one English graduate. It re-inforced what one knows, but tends to forget: that many adults have little acquaintance with children's literature, even of the most traditional kind, and also that even sensitive and intelligent adults working with children can be quite insensitive to children's literature. Finally, we selected twelve very different and individual people to join the team of fifteen librarians. Each one proved excellent, and made a very real contribution to the programme, as well as being conscientious and involved to a much greater degree than we had any right to expect. Added to the storytelling librarians, an equally varied and interesting group, the result was a very strong team of twenty-seven with a common approach, and the ability to work together. It is a tribute to the librarians in the programme that all of them welcomed having outsiders join the team, and also that they all helped to make them feel at home. We can see no end to the possibilities for involving a wide range of people in this programme to add to the richness and variety of storytelling. We now know the kind of people we need as recruits. They must be flexible, adaptable, sensitive, imaginative, and able to share our vision of the limitless opportunities the programme can offer, as well as our general approach to children.

Anyone without any of these characteristics can disrupt the programme and other members of the team, as was obvious one year
when for a short time our driver was an authoritarian teacher, unable
to cope with children except within the confines of a classroom, who
obviously disapproved of our casual approach, and after one
admittedly rowdy session, said indignantly that he thought staff
should get danger money for storytelling!

Naturally the team are vulnerable. They go into a park, and collect
a group of children who want to listen to stories. The team are as
much guests in the park as the children are, and have to accept what
comes. They can't say 'Leave the park' to anyone who decides to
play up. If children try to disconnect the equipment or run off with
the banner, this can be stopped unobtrusively by two of the team
who are quietly in the background keeping one step ahead of
potential troublemakers while the other storyteller is in action. The
first year our speaker was the funnel type, but this proved too
tantalizing, as it used to be filled with leaves or pebbles, so for the
second year we changed to a boxed-in model which was not such
an easy target. If there are children just making a noise, or moving
about, this does not matter, as the fact that a microphone is used
gives the storyteller the upper hand in almost any situation. There
is always a feeling of informality about sessions, and people feel free
to come and go as they please, but this need not distract those who
want to go on listening. Also, hecklers can be dealt with or ignored
according to the technique and temperament of each storyteller. Some
children enjoy hanging round the edge of the group making derisory
comments; others delight in giving away the climax as the storyteller is building up to it. The microphone is a help in such situations,
because whether the storyteller decides to engage in repartee or take
no notice, whatever he or she says predominates, just because it is
louder. Large groups can listen without straining, even if some of
them are a distance away, or many of them are restless. It has been
suggested that use of a microphone makes a storytelling session more
formal. I believe the opposite is true. The fact that the audience can
wriggle about, move or talk and still hear what is going on, creates a
natural and relaxed atmosphere, which is just what we want. I don't
want to imply that there are hecklers and disrupters at every session.

Nothing could be further from the truth. Some are miraculously quiet, with the entire audience listening; others are a complete riot, with hardly anyone listening. There are many reasons for this. Some stories are not as good as others; often something which interests them more is happening in the same area; or it may just be a cold or windy day, and children can't sit still for long. What is certain is that all of us experience good and bad sessions, often on the same day.

Almost invariably the stories we tell are traditional folk and fairy tales. I cannot put the familiar reasons for this more aptly than Frances Clarke Sayers does in the excellent chapter on *The Story-teller's Art* in her *Summoned by Books*:

The greatest source of literature for the storyteller lies readily at hand. It is folklore. Here are the stories which come ready-made to the tongue. These are the stories that existed before reading and writing were invented; and time and the storyteller's art have worn away all that was extraneous and unnecessary to the tale.

Our only stipulation is that stories should be selected from folk-tale collections we are prepared to stock in the library, so that the storyteller can show the books from which the stories come at the beginning of each session. What matters most is that everyone should make their choices from a wide background reading of folk-tales. An excellent preparation for this is to read Elizabeth Cook's *The Ordinary and the Fabulous*. Each year it is fascinating to see how people instinctively select stories which appeal to them and suit their personalities as well as their particular style of storytelling. Stories are learnt, although never strictly word for word. However this is done, and everyone develops their own method, it is essential to become so steeped in the story that it is almost instinctive to reproduce some of the most telling phrases and to retain the flavour of the language as well as the spirit of the tale when recreating the story afresh for each audience. I find learning stories a dreadful chore, as I have a notoriously bad memory. My method is to re-read the story many times, until I can easily visualize the plot. I then abandon attempts to reproduce the language, but try to describe the events of the story as I see them happening. I find it most helpful to do this aloud out-of-doors, and tend to choose a quiet time of day in a local park when I can walk up and down declaiming without attracting too much curiosity. When I can get through a story without faltering, at a more rapid pace than I will eventually tell it, I go back to the text and steep myself in it again, so that I can absorb some of the most vivid phrases and descriptions. Some people record themselves on tape, which they play over while doing the washing-up; others find it gives them most confidence to try out stories they are learning on children they know.

Selecting stories to tell is not as easy as it may sound. Collections of folk tales and fairy tales proliferate, but many of them are in versions too literary and over-written for telling. This is ironic. Such traditional tales were only written down after centuries of re-telling had stripped the language to the bare bones. Years of re-writing have in turn caused many of them to be ruined for telling. At one end of the scale there are powerful tales badly re-told in banal and over-descriptive language; at the other impeccably written tales in stilted or archaic language. Both categories would be equally disastrous and totally failing in impact if told aloud, though no doubt the latter are very pleasant to read, even if by the time many children are fluent enough to read them, they are past the stage of being interested in traditional tales anyway. However long it takes most of us to actually learn stories, much more time is spent reading through endless collections to find stories which both appeal to the storyteller and can be told aloud. Each of our team learns about six stories for the summer programme and we keep a central register, so that there is no duplication. Looking at the titles of the 160-odd stories told in 1972, is a fascinating exercise. Certain collections are well-used; supremely Joseph Jacobs, the Brothers Grimm, and the anthologies collected by Ruth Manning-Sanders, particularly *The Book of Giants* and *The Book of Ghosts and Goblins*; tales from Japan, China, Scandinavia, India, the West Indies and Africa; many unfamiliar stories, and also many old favourites like *Bluebeard, Rapunzel* and *Jack and the Beanstalk*: long stories like *The Princess of Tomboso* and short ones like *Lazy Jack*; a few modern stories like *How the Whale Became* by Ted Hughes, *The Elephant's Child* by Rudyard Kipling, and *The King who Declared War on the*

*Animals* by Joan Aiken. One thing is certain. The stories are as varied as the personalities of the storytellers. We have found it essential to learn a mixture of long and short, simple and complex stories; each session is a new experience, and every audience is different. We aim mainly at the seven to ten year olds; but in practice, the audience may well be from three to thirteen. Sessions are usually about twenty-five minutes, but are often slightly less or more according to the situation.

What are the sites we visit? We try to go anywhere where there are likely to be groups of children, so that sites include sports centres, parks, one of the open-air pools, adventure playgrounds, school play centres, play spaces and isolated housing estates. Each site is different. Play spaces tend to be more restless; parks more peaceful and idyllic. Nothing conveys the atmosphere better than the brief reports sent in by storytellers. Here is one from a temporary summer holiday play space:

The site was crowded—all ages. About a dozen children came to sit quietly and listen, followed later by several more, but a group of older children jeered, shouted, ran amongst them, hit them with branches, echoed the storyteller from a nearby tree, and were generally disruptive. The storyteller kept amazingly cool, a fact much appreciated by the few who managed to listen.

Nothing proves better how different each site is every week, and how totally unpredictable, than the next report from the same site:

Both storytellers apprehensive about this site after last week's report, but it went like a dream, with an audience of about forty listening with rapt attention.

The weather is the most unpredictable factor, but the teams carry on unless it is pouring with rain, as the following reports show:

Audience of 40–45. Fine breezy weather. Children (most youngish) braved the dust storms kicked up by the wind.

Audience of 12. Cold, spitting rain. Very few children about, but most came into the playground area, and listened with great concentration, some with coats over their heads, as the drizzle increased.

Audience of 12–25 fluctuating. A damp dark afternoon, intermittently showery. Smallish audience stood and sat expectantly, avoiding puddles in the playground—then the equipment wouldn't work, and it took all of that session

to repair a fuse—so stories were shouted at fairly mobile audience, with understandably, much audience participation. A heavy shower, and we moved under
the shelter to finish first story, which was fairly chaotic, as hecklers took advantage of the splendid echoes; outside again for second story, with a small core
of about 12 still interested and a restless fringe.

And perhaps the most forlorn of all, from a play space:

Audience of 25. We sat near the bonfire which was nice as it was quite cold.

When the weather is good, so are most sessions:

Audience of 110. Perfect situation, children running out of the pool to join
in – huge crowd, many mothers and fathers, almost everyone stayed for complete
session of about half an hour.

Audience of 60 plus. Large audience, some babies, particularly one in a
pram—several family groups, a few men and women on their own and three
teenagers with bikes—all lying in the sun nearby listening, as well as the large
intent group of children round the storyteller.

The parks in Lambeth vary a great deal. The most recent is
Larkhall Park, still in a fairly rudimentary state, as it was created
from an area of wasteland which had been left unattended for years:

Audience of 15. Problems—noise from railway, aeroplanes and demolition
works. Reception—very attentive, already waiting, pleased, eager for us to
return next week.

Slade Gardens is a small park, tucked away down a side street. We
rely there heavily on drawing audiences from the One O'clock Club
(intended for under fives, but in holiday periods crowded with older
children) and the play park area, as the following report shows:

Large audience, gathered from the play park and One O'Clock Club, some
still dressed up in lengths of curtain material . . . also some lads who came for
entertainment at our expense, if they could get it, but were soon involved in
deep discussion with the driver.

One of the sure sites is Clapham Common:

Audience of 70. The common was thick with children in every direction, so
Beulah visited both the fish pond and the swings to collect an audience. The
swings were straightforward, but at the fish-pond she asked what was being
used for bait and got a closer view than she bargained for. In addition to the

children there were numerous mothers, a few old men who strolled past, and a sprinkling of sleepy puppies in the audience. The children were extremely receptive and responded well.

## The lido in Brockwell Park is always interesting:

Audience of 12–20. Very attentive, mostly girls and of an age from 5–11 years. Storytelling took all the children from the pool! Again we were announced over the loud-speaker, and the fountain was turned off. With our equipment in the enclosed area of the lido the stories carried all round—so everyone heard. Good session.

## So is an official Council car park behind Brixton Library, which is clear of cars by 5.30 p.m., although we never managed to collect many children there:

Audience of 11. When we got there no children were in sight. We wandered up and down with the banner until a couple of kids came to see what was going on. They said they were not allowed to move from outside their homes, so I sent them to ask their mothers. Eventually we had a very attentive audience of 11 plus 4 bigger boys listening while playing games. Lots of adults passing by with bags of shopping stopped to listen.

## Reactions are endlessly varied, even in the course of the same afternoon:

Slightly restless session at tough school play centre, after which one boy achieved his ambition of shouting 'bugger' down the microphone fractionally before I switched off, and looked rather surprised when I didn't react at all. Later as I collected children in Ruskin Park, one exquisite young lady came up and asked how long the session would be. When told, she said primly, 'Oh, just about as long as my piano lessons.' Excellent session with a large number of family groups, and many regulars already waiting when we arrived at the site.

## It is interesting now to read the first report from a session on a housing estate, to which the storytellers moved when the adjacent play space proved unsuitable:

Children gathered from the fenced-off playground, and it was worth circum-navigating the various blocks of flats to gather children from the houses on the fringe of the estate. They were keen hecklers and excellent shots with peanuts, but we achieved good publicity not least because of the numerous adults on the balconies above. One elderly man, overhearing snatches of the story of Anansi preaching to the crabs, thought we were a group trying to persuade the children to go to church!

Our decision to include housing estates in the 1972 programme turned out to be one of the most challenging and interesting developments of all. In some of them, grim Victorian buildings with courtyards in the in the middle, children were cooped up, isolated and confined. The first time we went inside, they came up and asked which flat we were looking for. At first they were wary when we said we had come to tell stories. They wouldn't sit down, and came and went throughout the session. The idea of storytelling was unfamiliar:

Audience of 25. Young, interested and slightly bewildered—several mothers brought their children specially and were waiting when we arrived. Good session, kept short, as they were not used to stories and couldn't take much.

Audience of 70. Nearly all very attentive, they took a longer session than one would have thought and responded very well. Some listeners were much older than average. Others were watching us from balconies, too far away to hear, but concentrating intently on our activities. These sessions are much harder work, but I think we should intensify the number of visits. Many of the children here need to get used to us as people before they can concentrate on anything as sophisticated as a plot.

Audience size and atmosphere varied considerably:

Audience of 15 approx. plus 7–8 teenagers and 4 workmen who pretended they weren't listening, and one small disruptive element throwing stones but he calmed down. Competition from one terribly busy-buzzing-bee.

Audience of 80. In many ways a great session—most of the kids listened hard—but there were about 10 older boys sitting on the roof of the bicycle shed behind us making a din and throwing wet tea-bags (from the dustbins) at us. Also about 8 boys on bikes, honking their horns etc. A tough 25 minutes.

Audience of 12. Children under 7 years old attentive and appreciative. One resident thanked us for keeping the children quiet and gave us a cup of coffee. Not many children in evidence on the estate, most of the ones that were came to the session. The aforesaid resident asked if the storytellers were 'volunteers'— on being told we were librarians, he was amazed—'Didn't know librarians did things like that'.

And so to the last report of the summer:

Audience of about 40. What a superb, and challenging site this is. Hordes came and went, and a strong core stood incredibly still (the entire ground was littered by broken glass) and listened intently. Meanwhile one small boy tried to wind the mike cord round himself, another tried to get into the suitcase holding the equipment, another poked one of my toes with a twig, and about six cut off any possible retreat backwards by sitting on the railings behind me. A great session to end with – despite all distractions the inner group never stopped listening. They can soak up stories here.

As the reports show, not only children come to listen to stories. In the parks and on housing estates particularly, adults sometimes listen too. The storytelling teams are becoming recognized now as they travel about the borough, and few people are surprised to see the banner being carried around in the parks and play areas. One of the storytelling librarians wandered into a park one lunchtime, carrying several books, and planning to eat a sandwich as she brushed up on a story to tell later that afternoon. However, she was spotted by children who rushed up and asked if she had come to tell stories; she had to retreat into the nearest pub to find any peace and quiet. Certainly the programme has become familiar to adults who work in all the places we visit, as well as to many parents. We have established friendly relationships with many people we had never even met before this programme began. Staff in the parks, sports centres and play spaces know what we are trying to do, and give us every support. Going out with the storytelling team is enjoyable, not just because it is always a challenge and always interesting to tell stories to children, but also for the easy contact it gives us with other people.

Sometimes I am asked whether our summer storytelling programme has resulted in a marked increase in the use of libraries. I always reply that I neither know nor care. To think in such terms shows the questioner has completely failed to understand our purpose. Many of the children we meet are obviously starved of stories. There is something very sad about this. I remember the first year we began storytelling. I had consciously chosen unfamiliar and rather tough stories after looking round the parks at our potential audience. Walking through Brixton one day, I was stopped by a waif-like girl of about ten. 'Will you tell us *Cinderella* in Brockwell Park next week?' she asked. It might be reasonable to suppose that a ten-year-old would have had a surfeit of the most

familiar stories like *Cinderella*, and would have reached the stage
of needing something more sophisticated. But so many of the
children we meet in Lambeth have missed out on an essential stage
of childhood. No one at home has ever told them stories, hence the
fact that they still long to hear *Cinderella* at the age of ten. Many
children are not only starved of stories, but are totally unused to
just *listening*. The only visual aids they are given, are to see the book
from which each tale has come held up at the beginning of the story,
and also to be able to watch the storyteller. Every storyteller is
different, and favours a different approach. Some are dramatic,
others completely still and quiet, yet others have a compelling
presence. Variety is important, and every method is valid. What
matters is that each time a story is told it is recreated specially for
the audience who hear it. Let Kornei Chukovsky, writing about the
goal of the storyteller in *From Two to Five*, have the last word:

> It consists of fostering in the child, at whatever cost, compassion and humane-
> ness—this miraculous ability of man to be disturbed by another being's mis-
> fortunes, to feel joy about another being's happiness, to experience another's
> fate as one's own. Storytellers take trouble to teach the child in his early years
> to participate with concern in the lives of imaginary people and animals, and to
> make sure that in this way he will escape the narrow frame of his egocentric
> interests and feelings.
>
> Because it is natural for a child to be on the side of the kind, the courageous,
> and the unjustly offended when listening to a fairy tale, whether it is Prince
> Ivan or Peter Rabbit or the Fearless Spider, our only goal is to awaken, nurture
> and strengthen in the responsive soul of the child this invaluable ability to feel
> compassion for another's unhappiness and to share in another's happiness—
> without this a man is inhuman.

It may not always seem so, but ultimately that is part of what it is
all about.

# 5
# Book Selection

Book selection should never be considered in isolation. Generalizations about bookstocks as 'well rounded collections' are totally meaningless unless related to a total philosophy of librarianship. Book selection is one of the most vital aspects of librarianship, requiring a mixture of imagination, common sense, intelligence, firmness, organizing ability, professional skill, knowledge of children and books and awareness of the society within which the librarian operates. The selection of materials is the essence and cornerstone of librarianship, and if librarians fail in this respect then they are failures indeed.

No one responsible for the bookstock in a group of libraries can afford to be complacent. A clear-cut book selection policy is essential, but so is flexibility within that framework. Decisions have to be taken, and they are not always straightforward. A book selection policy cannot be even remotely logical unless it relates to a coherent philosophy of librarianship. In one sense, a philosophy is a necessary prop in selecting books, and it is obviously much harder to operate without it. One thing is certain. Book selection involves decision-making. No one can opt out. Books on the shelves of any library reveal something of the ideas or lack of ideas behind the selection. A parallel can be drawn with people who say they have not made up their minds about contemporary issues of conscience. There is no escape from such issues, and their non-committal comments reveal the choices they have made. Too many library shelf stocks show that the selection policy is based on the theory of 'if in doubt, buy a copy'. This nervous approach inevitably results in an anaemic collection of books and too few copies of the titles that matter most. You cannot have positive book selection without positive librarians.

Book selection should always be considered within the framework of the publishing situation. Over 2,000 children's books are published in England each year, of which approximately 1,500 are new titles. Although the figure dropped in 1971 from the total in 1970 for the first time in recent years, there is no reason to suppose that there will be a spectacular decrease in the near future. At the moment there are over 16,000 in print. Is it necessary to have so many children's books? Of course not. Just suppose a child during childhood (loosely defined for this purpose as ages two to twelve) absorbed two books a week throughout that period. The total is just over a thousand books. Obviously this crude example is full of loopholes, but at least it serves to point up the absurdity of the situation. Children should have a wide choice of books, but 16,000 titles is ridiculous. Why should so many be published? No publisher who builds up a children's list is likely to drastically reduce the number of titles published annually. There are now 87 publishers who belong to the Children's Book Group of the Publisher's Association. Some are long-established, with backlists of titles which show flair, integrity, imagination and skill on the part of publishers, writers and artists; others exist almost entirely on indifferent series publishing; many clearly leaped on the bandwagon in the first flush of excitement as school libraries began to develop, and have since floundered in a sea of mediocre books, because they have little hope of attracting the best writers who tend to be snapped up by the best publishers; still others patently have no concern except to make money. The absurd over-production of new books yields an annual crop which can be divided almost without exception into a number of broadly defined categories: those which are truly creative and exciting; those which are serviceable and useful; those which are remarkably chiefly for packaging, being both tasteful and beautifully produced, but of little substance (a group which seems to increase every year); those which are mediocre and instantly forgettable (always a very large group); and those cynically and shoddily produced for the mass market. There are naturally some wonderful books about which it is possible to enthuse, but it is supremely important for anyone involved in book selection to cultivate an attitude of healthy scepticism and a robust sense of humour both of which are essential aids to selection. Librarians should never be taken in by books. The evidence on library shelves points to the fact that many librarians are inexcusably gullible.

How can librarians keep up with the flood of new books? Book selection is essentially a group activity, and should give opportunities for discussion arising out of the books under review. I feel that it is valuable at least to see almost everything that is published. The worst books can be dismissed after a glance, but it helps to be continually reminded how bad some of them are. Obviously the most satisfactory method of seeing the new books is to have them supplied regularly on approval by a bookseller, although many libraries will not be able to follow this system. In Lambeth we meet every two weeks, when we have a delivery of new titles. For about two hours we look at the books, and then discuss them. Many of the rejects only take a few minutes to dispose of, several books choose themselves, and picture books can be read on the spot. Other books which need to be read before a decision is made are taken away and reported on at the next meeting. Inevitably at peak publishing times in the year, because there are far more books to consider each fortnight, they all receive less attention. I know the views of publishers about the Christmas book trade, and the rush to publish books in the Autumn, but so far as libraries are concerned, the *average* book has a better chance of being *fairly* considered for purchase if it is published in February rather than October. I doubt that any library system can afford to double the time allowed for book selection, which would probably be necessary to cope with the flood of Autumn books if they are to be given as much attention as those published throughout the rest of the year. The most outstanding books almost select themselves, and many of the rejects are obvious at a glance, but the more ordinary titles are likely to be passed over if published during this busy period. Naturally there are books which will sell particularly well just before Christmas, but need publishers also launch at this time the kind of serviceable books which will hardly cause a ripple, and are unlikely to be purchased as presents by even the most uninitiated buyer of children's books?

Group discussion about books can be extremely valuable. In any library system there are bound to be some staff with longer experience than others, as well as some with a surer instinct for selecting books;

yet others will have been given a better groundwork in book selection during their time at library school, as no one could claim that all schools of librarianship are equal. Staff will learn as much from each other, and more readily, than they will from whoever co-ordinates the book selection. A practising children's librarian will inevitably have a better day to day knowledge of how children are currently responding to books, which is important. A supervising librarian on the other hand will not be in as close touch with today's children, but will have the experience to exercise the checks and controls that are essential. It takes time to have read enough to develop a sound judgement.

American librarians are sometimes politely amazed at the hap-hazard way English librarians are expected to build up a knowledge of books. As far as I know, no English library system has as rigorous an in-service training programme as many American libraries where newly-qualified librarians are expected to read, assess and report on a specific number of books per week for a considerable period of time. The situation here has been thrown into sharper relief by the speeded-up training of librarians. In the days when it was customary to work in a library for several years before going to library school, or when librarians qualified by part-time study, it was possible to become quite well-read (although it certainly didn't always happen!) in a reasonably leisurely way over a long period of time. The old-style children's librarian would get many opportunities to read during slack periods at the counter. In my own case, I worked as an assistant in a very un-busy library for two years, and read intensively, which proved an invaluable groundwork for my knowledge of children's books. It is much harder for the young qualified librarian today. Certainly this is true in Lambeth, and other systems where librarians are relieved from the tedium of clerical counter duties, and are involved in a wide range of activities. No one would wish on them the drudgery experienced by librarians under the old system, but I think that supervising librarians should consider as a matter of some urgency how this problem of reading widely can be tackled in a systematic way.

Anyone who is ever satisfied either with the methods of selection or the stock on the shelves must have limited goals. Book selection should always be a case of striving for perfection, but also knowing that it will never be achieved. Whatever the book selection policy, there will be paradoxes which it is never possible to completely resolve. For example, no one could deny that the balance between providing books which are in demand, but also making available books which might be read if they were there, is complicated. It is a waste of money to buy books which are totally out of touch with children for whatever reason. Of course, it can be a disastrously limiting thing to say too glibly 'I don't think anyone will read this book, therefore we should not buy it'. It is pointless to give shelf space to books which do not go out, but it is a failure to understand what book selection is about if a stock is confined to what is known to be read.

Fortunately library book funds are not limitless, and this at least prevents the wastage of ratepayer's money which would be inevitable if timid librarians with no clearly defined policy could spend as much as they liked. In view of the over-production of new books, even those librarians who practice the theory 'if in doubt, buy a copy' have limited scope. However, every book bought means one that can't be bought. I could name a library system in London in which most novels above a certain price level appear to be purchased. Scrutinizing the shelves in several of their branch libraries, as I once had the opportunity to do, I found a wide range of the mediocre books published during the past few years, but learned that they had to take reserves for *Mary Poppins* and *The Wind in the Willows* because there were only two copies of each title per branch. Now this does not make sense. Surely a saturation policy (that is, ensuring that there are always copies of certain titles on the shelves) should be a first essential for popular and good books which have survived the passage of time?

There are two important facts to remember about children's library stock. One is that books are intended for use, and most of them will wear out quickly. The other is that children *keep being born*. It is not just that at any one time many children will be seizing *The Lion, the Witch and the Wardrobe* or rushing to the books on judo or dinosaurs; each year new generations will be discovering them. New books matter, but old books matter even more, and a greater proportion of staff time should be spent on revision of the existing stock than on the selection of new books. I dislike glib generalizations about book funds, but it is probably true to say that a library system with a reasonable allocation of money will spend about two-thirds of it annually on replacements, and one third on new books.

Stock revision should be continuous, and requires skill; however, the bulk of replacements in a children's library require no more skill than that of a supermarket manager who ensures that certain brands of coffee and soup and a varied selection of cheeses are always available. In other words, the demand for certain titles and categories of books is utterly predictable, and there should be a system to take care of this automatically so that librarians are freed to concentrate on replacing stock which requires individual attention. The life of the average picture book in a library is not likely to be more than at most six months. A picture book which issues twenty times before it has to be withdrawn has done well. It stands to reason that because picture books as a category are in heavy demand, they will need to be continually re-ordered at each service point. It does not make sense to repeat orders, possibly for the same titles, month after month at different service points. Bulk purchases of multiple copies is the only satisfactory answer. In Lambeth we have compiled a  list of the picture books we are prepared to stock in bulk. Automatically every month, twelve copies of a specific number of titles from this list are bought. They are stored in a reserve collection, and as staff need more picture books at any service point they visit the reserve collection, and help themselves to whatever they need. There are nearly five hundred titles on the picture book list, which is revised every year, when books which are out of print or have gone dead are weeded out, and the best publications of the past year are added. Probably about half the titles on the list will be represented in the reserve stock at any one time, so that there is always a fair degree of choice. Because more titles are ordered automatically every month, and the turnover is rapid, all titles on the list are ordered reasonably often. In addition to the picture book list, there are also separate lists of traditional folk and fairy tales, nursery rhymes, easy readers and a short list of standard fiction. Reserve stocks are built up in exactly the same way as for the picture book list. As the standard fiction list is short, every title on it is represented all the time. If it is discovered at any service point that there is no copy of *Tom Sawyer* or *The Borrowers* on the shelf, the daily van delivery should remedy this immediately. This system requires both sufficient storage space and an adequate book fund. However, there is no doubt it is the most economic and satisfactory way of coping with these specific categories. Once they are taken care of in what becomes nothing more than a clerical operation, staff can concentrate their time and skill on the rest of the stock.

Because books are being used all the time, and the child population is changing all the time, librarians should never stop revising and replacing stock. A children's library stock can deteriorate rapidly in three months if it is not given constant attention. The housewife can never stock up on tinned food and then forget about it for six months. Some of it will need replacing continually, all of it in time. The same is true of books. I believe very strongly that library books should be clean and should look bright and attractive. Those which are in poor physical condition should be removed from the shelves. In Lambeth we have virtually stopped binding children's books over the past five years or so, and we never bind a book which cannot be rebound incorporating the laminated jacket, as a heavy binding kills a book stone-dead as far as most children are concerned. This is understandable, because modern children expect library books to have laminated jackets; also a heavy binding may re-inforce the book, but it also re-inforces the fears of the many children defeated by lack of fluency in reading to whom a book is a formidable object.

It must be obvious that I do not see the librarian who works with children as primarily a preserver or custodian of books, but I do believe that someone should be concerned with preserving children's books in a more systematic way than by the spasmodic little collections of old children's books being built up in different places. I admit to casting very envious glances at the superb reference collection of children's books in New York Public Library, now housed in the new Central Children's Room at Donnell Library Centre. When I was in New York in 1963, I worked for several

months in the Central Children's Room, then in the Fifth Avenue
Library. I remember vividly the kind of queries which came up
daily. For example, a modern dance company, about to stage a
version of Andersen's *The Princess and the Pea* wanted to look at all
illustrated editions of Andersen to get ideas for the set; on another
occasion, a man writing an article on Robert Louis Stevenson
needed to compare editions of *Treasure Island*. In both cases, the
library was able to produce a bewildering range and variety of
editions old and new, from throughout the world. This was only
because the foresight and determination of Anne Carroll Moore
caused her to start this collection which her successors were inspired
to carry on. However, it was also practice in New York Public
Library to build up mammoth reference collections of 'good
literature' in every branch library of a reasonable size, which struck
me as a chronic waste of money, as well as an indulgence on the part
of the staff who tended to make far more use of these collections
than ever the children did. Although in New York they undoubtedly
over-emphasized the preservation element in the bookstock to the
detriment of the readers, we tend to have been inexcusably casual
in this country about our children's books. Considering the long
history of children's books in England, it is significant that many of
the best examples of our early books are in places like New York
Public Library, Philadelphia Free Public Library and, supremely,
in the Osborne Collection in Canada. I am afraid no one could
quarrel with the wisdom of Edgar Osborne in sending his magnificent
collection abroad to be preserved. I well remember in my early days
as a children's librarian that the collection of early children's books
acquired by YLG (and now housed at The Department of Librarianship, Manchester Polytechnic) was kept in a state of total disorder
in cardboard boxes at the Library Association. I was approached by
some of the elders of the profession at that time, who although they
did not express it quite like that, obviously thought that my energies
would be best channelled into cataloguing this random collection!
I declined, as I had vowed that once I had managed to pass those
dreary exams in cataloguing and classification (at the third attempt!)
I would never voluntarily catalogue or classify another book. It
would be nice to think that if in future years a scholarly social

historian wanted to bring up to date Harvey Darton's magnificent *Children's Books in England* which ends at the turn of the twentieth century, he would be able to draw on a wealth of easily accessible and carefully preserved material in a number of major libraries. This becomes more important as children's books now go out of print so rapidly. I must admit, however, that my own primary interest is today's children, not yesterday's books.

The increasing frequency with which children's books go out of print is tiresome from the librarian's point of view. So often even books which are useful, individual, and read by children have a very short life. I remember a publisher from a rather mediocre publishing house visiting Lambeth. She asked eagerly how popular the novels she published were in Brixton. I showed her the few we had bought, all sitting on the shelves. Then, as she began to look depressed, I fortunately spotted one which was rarely in—an attractive and appealing story, an instant success with children. 'Oh dear,' she said 'that's just going out of print.' There is scope for much co-operation here between librarians and publishers, and it was interesting recently that the Bodley Head sent out a circular letter to librarians before deciding which of a number of their children's books to reprint, and had a very good response to the questions they asked.

The fact that publishers often cannot afford to reprint good books which should be on the shelves of any self-respecting library reflects badly on librarians. There is always an element of risk and a degree of decision-making in buying new books. Replacing books should involve quite as much, if not more, experience and skill, but stock replacement can be a sinecure for the lazy-minded or insecure librarian. Many library shelves give the unmistakable impression that the replacement policy is 'if it is still in print, buy it again'. Two groups of people suffer from this approach: the readers and the best publishers. Perhaps the most serious result is that we are failing to support publishers with real integrity, and are helping to encourage the slipshod and shoddy publishing of second-rate books. We complain bitterly about mediocre books. Any library supplier will provide unmistakable evidence that many librarians continue to buy them. No wonder that publishers sometimes privately despair of librarians. Ruthlessness is a first essential in book selection. There should be a good reason for buying every book. The fact that a book has been previously in stock is never sufficient justification for buying it again, but those books which are proven and good should be replaced in quantity.

Few things irritate me more than the suggestion that publishers are or should be influenced by librarians as a gauge of how far writers should be allowed to go, when dealing with subjects which are either delicate or taboo. The idea that librarians should set themselves up as arbiters of moral standards, and the implication that they are like old-fashioned maiden aunts pursing their lips at the hint of homo-sexuality or rude words, are equally repellent. However, librarians could quite justifiably have much more influence than they have in the matter of refusing to buy second-rate books. Take the example of non-fiction series publishing, which has bedevilled children's books for so long. Can we entirely escape the blame? I think not. Some series books are excellent; others fulfil a need for a time; yet others should never be bought by anyone with the minimum training in book selection at all. Series publishing is beneficial to the publishers. Set up a series, and it can keep going for ever and a day. Establish a standard at first, and then slip in books of varying standards; timid selectors of books will sink thankfully into selecting books which at least all *look* the same—the dodges are obvious. Naturally, there are positive advantages, not least that an unusual book which would not be an economic proposition as a single title can sometimes be slipped into a series, but, there seems to me no better way of undermining the view that books are individual and different and unique, than to be confronted with endless books in series. Look at library shelves. They are stiff with series, although admittedly there are subjects on which there are *only* series books, and decisions then have to be made whether to have a series book or none at all—the kind of decision about which it is impossible to generalize, because it will depend on such factors as the importance of the subject and the quality of the series. Look at the series titles of many of those published over the past ten to fifteen years—patronizing and didactic and uninspired, they are calculated to induce boredom ... *The Young Specialist Looks at ...; Young*

*Person's guide to ...; Instructions to Young ...; Young Pathfinder's Library ...; Young Enthusiast's Library* (the latter is still my favourite!). Fortunately most of them can be dispensed with, but I am sure there are libraries where they will go on being replaced for some time to come, in common with a badly outdated series, *The Young Traveller in ...* which I recently saw well-represented on the shelves in the central children's library of one of the largest cities in the country.

There is no way to keep a stock live, other than by continually scrutinizing the shelf stock, and then re-looking at virtually every book, comparing old books with newly published ones, before making decisions about which titles to buy again. Obviously this is not always possible in practical terms, but it is the ideal at which to aim. Even in London there is no one place you could go to see everything you might want to buy. Our staff regularly visit library suppliers and bookshops to select replacements. It is interesting to watch staff who come fresh to selecting children's books. As part of their first exercise, they spend time looking at specific sections of stock (non-fiction, as it is obviously easier) at perhaps one service point, making notes on the subject gaps to be filled. Then they visit a library supplier with a large exhibition stock to try and fill the gaps. They arrive full of purpose, and are invariably disappointed by the inadequacies and limitations of children's books. Because here is the paradox. Certainly there are far too many children's books published each year, and too many in print at any one time. Certainly the outdated books can be weeded from library shelves, and only the best new ones bought. And yet it is still true that any moderately intelligent person who has worked with children in a library for six months, knows that children's books in some respects maddeningly fail to reflect the known interests and capabilities of children. Just consider all those detailed historical novels aimed at 'older children', most of whom if they read at all, certainly don't read historical novels; or the necessary subjects on which there are no books and the books on subjects which are totally unnecessary. Look at one category of books—biographies. There are adults who read biographies as a category, just as they might read travel books. The same is not generally true of children. Their reading of biographies is almost invariably related to school projects, and the dreary injunction to 'find out' about Helen Keller or Charles I. I don't think this need be so to the extent that it is, but a glance at biographies written for children explains part of the answer. The majority of them currently in print, at a rough count, are of nine-teenth-century famous people; they are nearly all English, with the exception of such universal figures as Leonardo da Vinci, Marie Curie, Louis Pasteur and Garibaldi; most of them are good project fodder; few are of living people, few even of people who died after 1950, which is over twenty years ago, and therefore as remote as the Elizabethans to a ten-year-old. By contrast, adult biographies have become ridiculously instant, and people of small significance inflict their life stories on the world before they are fifty. Naturally, some famous people are not ideal subjects for biographies for younger children. There was one, now out of print, of Edmund Kean, which was surely a strange choice. Neatly glossing over his drinking and womanizing, the actor was diminished, and the book was distinctly boring. Surely there are people in this century, both living and dead, whose lives could be of interest to modern children, other than Sir John Cockcroft, Lady Baden-Powell, Dag Hammarskjold, Sir Winston Churchill, Maria Montessori and Sir Mortimer Wheeler (a not unfair sample of the biographies available). It would be easy to make deductions both about British insularity and adult didacticism towards children from a study of the lives selected to put before them. So many children's books on factual subjects do not relate to the world children know, and it makes the task of the librarian trying to persuade children that books *do* relate to life extremely hard.

The muddle children's books are in is not really surprising. Very few publishers know what other publishers are producing. The best ones do, but they are a small number of the total. I should hate to see a situation in which publishers only published what librarians or teachers thought was needed, or filled in subject deficiencies proved by market research. There must be an element of spontaneity about publishing, but there is no doubt that in this country at the moment the publishing of children's books is too gloriously hap-hazard. So much is based on guesswork; no real research is done— and there is infinite scope for intelligent research. Adults write, illustrate, publish, and review children's books, also sell them in bookshops and buy them for libraries. This can be done without reference to children. It would be ingenuous to suggest (as is sometimes done, always with an air of discovery) that children should review or even write books for children; but on the other hand children should not be ignored. The result is too much wastage. One of my ambitions is to stage an exhibition called *Books a child of the Seventies could grow up without.* It would be a large exhibition and extremely easy to pick the books.

Just as publishing is too haphazard, so is the size of stock in most children's libraries. What determines the size? Often nothing more scientific than the resolve to fill the shelves with books. How is the number of shelves determined? Contrary to the impression generally given in library textbooks, it is obvious from looking at actual libraries that it is frequently based on the theory that all blank walls in the room should be filled with books. And how is the size of the room determined? In most cases it will naturally be determined by the size of the entire library site, which is hardly ever a matter of choice, but usually a case of accepting the space it has been possible to acquire to build—at least this is likely to be so in built-up urban areas. It is futile to generalize about the size of an ideal bookstock. So many factors must be taken into consideration—for example the size and type of community served, proximity to the adult bookstock, and its relationship to other libraries in the area. What is certain is that once the theories have been thrashed out, the bookstock should be selected based on the theories, and only then is it possible to say how much shelving will be required. In Lambeth we have found it necessary to reduce the shelving in many of our libraries just because they were built and filled with wall shelving, without taking into account the appropriate shelf stock likely to be needed. If there is too much shelving, there is a tendency to buy unnecessary or second-rate books just because empty shelves inevitably give the impression that there is a shortage of books in that particular library. For example, there are many libraries in the borough where very few children are capable of reading the long literary novels which are published, even if they wanted to. Although there must always be a wide enough choice for children to be able to stretch and grow in their reading, it is absurd to fill shelves with such books just for them to be transferred somewhere else in two years time because they have never been borrowed. After weeding a fiction shelf stock (which should be a regular activity) and withdrawing or transferring books which have gone dead, it is a common experience for staff to be anxious to fill up the shelves with live books. However, after selecting titles, and avoiding those which never issue, they are invariably surprised to find what a small core of books they have bought. The shelf stock is vitally important, because it indicates the range of choice available at any one time, but it is pointless to make it so wide that the same titles stand there day after day and are never borrowed. Stock revision should always be done from the bookstock. As mentioned previously, we have no catalogues in the children's libraries, and no adult fiction catalogues either. What is the purpose of a catalogue? All that it does is tell you that a book was once in stock. It is no help in actually *finding* the book, which may be on loan to a reader, withdrawn from stock but not yet crossed off in the catalogue, or missing without trace, to name only a few of the most obvious possibilities. The turnover of books in a children's library is rapid, and probably amounts to at least a third of the stock each year, with popular and much handled categories like easy readers lasting at the very most for nine months. Unless a great amount of staff time is spent in making additions and deletions to the catalogue, it is certain to give an inaccurate picture of the *actual* stock. *The British National Bibliography* covers all books published in this country from 1950 to date, so that catalogues are not needed to trace bibliographical details of books published within that period. Titles can also be traced in the annual *British Books in Print, Children's Books in Print* and *Paperbacks in Print.* So what point is there in all the work involved in maintaining catalogues? If a reader requests a book which is not on the shelf, and it is one we are prepared to supply (inevitably there are titles we will not supply because they have been rejected at book selection meetings, fall below our standards, or are in categories it is not our policy to stock), that title is added to a daily list of books requested at all libraries. The list is circulated, and each library checks its shelf stock on the same day for all requested titles. Those which are found

Storytelling indoors

Storytelling out-of-doors

are collected daily, and delivered to the requesting library. As far as children's books are concerned, this satisfies approximately seventy per cent of our requests. If the outstanding requests are still in print, and are titles we are prepared to duplicate even if we know they are already likely to be in stock (although obviously all out on loan at the time the shelves were checked), a phone call is made to a bookseller who does a shelf stock check in the bookshop, and is usually able to supply about half of them immediately. The others are ordered through a library supplier, which inevitably takes several weeks. Titles which are out of print, or which are probably in stock, but we are not prepared to replace, usually because they are too dated, are checked in the issues of the neighbourhood libraries which still use the Browne system of charging, in which it is possible to trace titles of books out on loan, and they are marked in the issue so that the request can be satisfied when they are returned. There used to be a master author catalogue maintained at the cataloguing section solely for the purpose of recording the stock number given to each book bought. It was never referred to by anyone except the staff of that section, or by the auditors who on their routine visits some-times try to trace specific books. Fortunately it has now been possible to persuade them that it is enough to note on the copy of each in-voice supplied with books, the stock numbers given to the books listed on that invoice. The invoices are then filed, and any auditor foolhardy enough to want to find an individual stock number has to plough through stacks of invoices until he eventually finds the number he is looking for.

Perhaps the over-riding advantage of not having catalogues is that staff can't use them as a prop. It means that staff have to get to know the stock well, and also use bibliographies intelligently.

Book selection and stock revision are continuous processes. Care of the bookstock is essentially a group activity, and like so many other things, a question of balance. Because librarians never do any real research either into what books children want to read, selection is based on a number of factors, which include use of the stock at various service points in so far as this can be determined. I introduce this tentative note just to show how arbitrary may be the conclusions we draw from this. What does it mean to say that a book issued five times last year? It means that on the evidence of the date stamps inside the book (provided a charging system which involves date stamps is used) five people officially borrowed that book from the library. How do we know any one of them really wanted to read it? We don't know. It could have been borrowed for a variety of reasons. Perhaps it was a book someone came specifically to get. On the other hand, it may have been a random choice, borrowed because it was there. Or was it taken as a substitute for a book which was wanted and wasn't there? How do we know any of the people who borrowed it read it? We don't know. Every question begs more. Issues are a very crude instrument of measurement, and should always be seen in perspective.

If as librarians we believe our job is to act as custodian to a neat, well-balanced collection of good children's books the task is reasonably easy. If we believe that the librarian and the bookstock should be reaching out into the community and should relate to that community, the task is much harder.

If the libraries are for all people, are we interested in helping those people who need it most begin where their interests are, with the sort of reading they can do, confident that they will progress?

Are we as librarians mortgaged to the power order that is, dispensing our books in the four walls to those who come, or can the library be a vital dynamic institution here in the swirling vortex of change?

This heady rhetoric comes from Dan Dodson, Director for Human and Community Studies, New York University, speaking at the American Library Association Conference in 1967. He asks good questions. If our answer is in the affirmative, what are the implications? Surely it means that we must try to find ways of making material for children with reading problems imaginatively and unobtrusively available. Book selection may be a question of balance, but should a bookstock be well balanced? In such a situation it is necessary to have a very *unbalanced* collection, in that a proportionately large amount of money will have to be spent on books which *are* easy to read; it means having a saturation policy for football books as well as for fairy tales; it means having some kind of policy in relation to writers like Enid Blyton. I make no apologies for introducing such a well-worn topic. Although her name is undoubtedly fading in fashionable areas, she will still be a talking point in many parts of the country for some time to come. This is always brought home to me every time I talk to groups of parents. Whatever the situation, I am always bound to be asked for my views on Enid Blyton. Recently, I made some mildly disparaging remarks about her in a BBC broadcast, which led to a number of highly indignant letters. She is fortunately an unrepeatable phenomenon, best analysed recently by E. W. Hildick in his *Children and Fiction*. No one writer could now dominate the publishing scene as she did in her day. Understandably, many if not most children go through a Blyton phase. After all, the plots have a strong appeal, until realization dawns that they are all the same. Many libraries refuse to buy Blyton books. I don't think this is a very helpful attitude, but if a library provides them in such quantity that there are always Blyton titles on the shelves, some children will continue to borrow them in preference to anything else. Because the vocabulary in all Blyton books is so limited, reading them presents no challenge to those who find reading difficult. This fact is often overlooked by people who glibly claim that children will *easily* pass through the Blyton phase. In Lambeth we buy only three of the most popular series. A small selection of titles is bought for each library, and complete sets of the same series are bought for a reserve stock. There are not enough titles in each library for them to sit on the shelves, but children frustrated by rarely finding any, can reserve specific titles, which will be supplied direct from reserve stock, and returned to it when the request has been satisfied. This same principle is applied to other popular series which are in great demand.

We should have above all, an acute awareness of our tendency as librarians to select books *we* want children to read rather than books children themselves want to read. This attitude can be justified in so far as librarians use professional skills in selecting and rejecting books, and also in introducing books to children. Discrimination and taste need to be developed, and sensitive guidance can be valuable. To suggest that children left to themselves will seek out the best is, apart from anything else, to overlook the sophisticated commerical interests dedicated to marketing the products to which children will be most vulnerable. The argument that to deprive children of the most excruciating television programmes churned out for them, because *they enjoy them so*, is the worst kind of sentimentality. Take the example of Walt Disney. In his fascinating book *The Disney Version*, Richard Schickel writes of the Disney machine:

> All its parts—movies, television, book and song publishing, merchandising, Disneyland—interlock and are mutually reciprocating. And all of them are aimed at the most vulnerable portion of the adult's psyche—his feelings for his children. If you have a child, you cannot escape a Disney character or story even if you loathe it. And if you happen to like it, you cannot guide or participate in your child's discovery of its charms. The machine's voice is so pervasive and persuasive that it forces first the child, then the parent, to pay it heed—and money. In essence, Disney's machine was designed to shatter the two most valuable things about childhood—its secrets and its silences—thus forcing everyone to share the same formative dreams.

Disney was an extreme example, who controlled a vast empire which lives on and flourishes after him. His treatment of the children's books he made into films, and the manner in which he falsified, trivialized and sentimentalized such books as *Mary Poppins* is depressing. Many less well-known individuals and organizations are engaged in similarly lucrative enterprises and their mass-produced books and wares can be seen on show in newsagents and chain stores. Children have much easier access to buying them than they are ever likely to have to real books (even paperbacks) unless there is a revolution in the book trade and it becomes as easy to buy children's books as it is to buy sweets or toys. Librarians should be realistic about what they are up against.

We should constantly review our attitudes to such questions as our policy towards abridged and re-written versions of full-length books. My own view is that re-written versions of famous books have no value. *Wuthering Heights* in basic English is no use to anyone. To de-vitalize the language of a great book is to show a total misunderstanding of what literature is about. *Cinderella* as retold in the *Ladybird* series is a third-rate experience. On the other hand, a good case can be made for some skilfully abridged versions of rather archaic children's books, like the version of *The Water Babies* edited by Kathleen Lines, which cuts out the tedious moralizing to which Charles Kingsley was prone.

To go back to Dan Dodson. 'If the libraries are for all people . . .'
Commitment to this ideal involves awareness of minority groups in
the community and a recognition of what this means in terms of
bookstock. We live in a multi-racial society. Would a stranger be
able to glean this fact from looking at library shelves? It is not enough
in an area with many children whose parents came from the West
Indies, India or Pakistan, to stock the small number of good books
for children on those countries. There must be enough copies for
them to be *seen* to be there.

Also, we need to be aware of our inbuilt standards as librarians in
relation to book production. It is sad but inevitable that whenever
books begin to be published to cater for specific minority needs,
they do not, to put it mildly, *look* as good as the general run of books.
When books for children with reading difficulties first began to be
published in Britain they were flimsy, and looked shoddy and
second rate, more like mean little textbooks than anything else.
Years ago, I remember going to great lengths to have collections of
them bound before being put into stock. Nowadays this would seem
to me unecessary. I believe it is important to have double standards
as far as book production is concerned. I would reject a flimsy book
on a subject which is well-covered bibliographically, whereas I would
consider it very important to buy Phyllis and Bernard Coard's
*Getting to Know Ourselves*, which is essentially a stapled booklet in
what would be considered an awkward format from a library point
of view. There is sure to be an increase in the production of such
booklets by minority groups or individuals without the resources of
a publishing house behind them, which libraries will need to stock.

The same is true of paperbacks. It is hardly news that children,
like teenagers, will borrow books in paperback which they would
not touch in hardback editions. Because of this fact, it seems to me
that arguments about the short life of paperbacks, or the suggestion
that they are an uneconomic proposition for libraries because of the
cost of processing and adding them to stock, are invalid, if we are
serious about encouraging people to read. In fact, without any
strengthening (and to bind a paperback is to make it more like a
hardback, and so defeat its psychological value) paperbacks will
last quite a few issues. And surely it is more sensible to simplify

the method of adding them to stock and processing them rather than fail to buy them for this reason? First things first. But then, this matter of standards in book production is another paradox. There was a time when children's books were very badly produced. Great efforts were rightly made to remedy the situation. Now many quality children's books have become so discreetly tasteful in appearance that even to look at the jackets induces instant boredom in those of us who have to handle them frequently. So how must children feel? The child who finds books unapproachable and formidable has this view confirmed. The gulf between writing at both ends of the reading market is re-inforced by the *appearance* of books at both ends of the market. So many children's books look exclusive, lack the common touch. I would no more want to see all children's books looking like the cheapest and shoddiest ones than I would want all children's books written in basic English. But they could well *look* less rarefied. (Just as some of the writers whose books adults enjoy analysing at conferences would do well to consider that children actually read novels for the *story*, not for the characterization, the descriptive passages, the fine writing or the psychological implications.)

A collection of quality English children's books gives an over-all impression as unreal and as conventional as a photograph of a trendy bathroom designed for those elusive readers of Sunday colour supplements who are assumed both to be furnishing an entire house from scratch, and lacking in sufficient initiative to decide on a colour scheme. Books are for use. They should *look* as if they are. Some publishers have developed a house style to the extent that all their full-length novels look exactly the same in format, type, layout and frequently also style of jacket illustration. Seen together, they look like series books, and there is an air of remoteness about them which does not help the child who is wary of books. Naturally I do not believe that children should only be confronted with what is familiar to them, but is it any wonder that most children will seize on paperbacks for preference, particularly a series like *Topliners*, with their generously large type and photographic jackets which instantly relate to the worlds of television, films and everyday images which are familiar to *all* children? Sometimes

I am forced to the unmistakable conclusion that certain publishers must have a professional death-wish. Communication is an over-used but very relevant word in our time. Some books seem deliberately designed to re-inforce the view that they are either obsolete, or sacred objects, and certainly are not for handling. I find myself wondering who these books are for? Can it be that somewhere there are hordes of children totally unlike any of those I have come across in my personal and professional life?

'Are we as librarians mortgaged to the power order that is, dispensing our books in the four walls to those who come, or can the library be a vital dynamic institution here in the swirling vortex of change?' asks Dan Dodson. I like the phrase 'mortgaged to the power order that is'. As far as children's books are concerned, there isn't much opportunity of showing that we are anything else. Apart from making a token gesture by displaying copies of *The Little Red Schoolbook*—that is about the extent of it. I am reminded of the delightful (and true) story of the puzzled Cuban visitor to the 1970 Children's Book Show, who asked a Lambeth librarian on duty there where he could find the left-wing children's books! Seriously, seen in isolation, children's books are deeply old-fashioned and very conservative. It was a challenge recently for us to try and think of any books which would seem appropriate to send for a display at a working conference on *Alternatives to Education*.

Fortunately, though, a children's bookstock does not exist in isolation, but in relation to the adult bookstock. One of the most important things about breaking down barriers between work with children and adults is that the stock in both departments should be extremely flexible and easy of access. There are subjects on which there is no need for children's books, except at the very simplest level. Examples are cookery and bird identification. Also, many adults would enjoy some children's novels, particularly historical ones, more than children, so why shouldn't they be put in adult collections?

Naturally there will be most interchange at the level of young adults, although it should be superflous to say, on the basis of all that has been said, experienced, and written about this subject in the United States, that this should be seen to come from the adult, not

the children's side. Undoubtedly where children's and adult collections are housed in geographically separated departments, there
will need to be duplication of some material in both collections. To
use the previously quoted examples, the *Good Housekeeping New
Basic Cookery*, *Collins Pocket Guide to British Birds* and the books
of Paul Zindel should be duplicated in both.

It is a very interesting development that the Bodley Head recently
took the initiative in trying to break down the similarly rigid barriers
which exist in publishing between children's and adult books, by
such moves as their special imprint *Books for New Adults* and by the
deliberately ambiguous *Bodley Head Archaeologies* which have not
been designed specifically either for children or adults.

Many of the frustrations and limitations of children's books
should not be apparent in adult bookstocks. However, it is sad that
most public libraries show little visible proof that they are aware of
the contemporary world, or that they cater for the reading interests of
the under twenty-fives. Compare the stock of a live contemporary
bookshop with the average public library shelves, and the latter
almost invariably look as if the stock was frozen into position at the
latest about 1950. Few libraries seem even to acknowledge the
existence of the most established underground literature. One gets
the impression, in London at least, that it is considered fairly daring
to subscribe to *Time Out*. Take the vital question of black literature
collections. Despite the wealth of written material which almost
daily points to the importance of establishing such collections,
English librarians still tend to take refuge in arguments which belong
to the thinking about race relations of five to ten years ago, and
supremely fail to recognize that the days for mouthing mild liberal
sentiments about balanced collections, and the dangers of establishing separate sections of the bookstock are long past. As schools begin
to engage in Black Studies, there is an increasing demand for
relevant material in libraries. Again, it is not enough to stock
relevant materials. There must be enough for them to be *seen* to be
there. It is a terrifying failure of imagination not to realize, in view
of the evidence, the situation we are in. It should be patently obvious
to any sensitive person who is white and British that in the face of
the betrayals and prejudice experienced by black people in this

country, and the racism of our recent legislation, we should seize every opportunity, not just to redress the balance, but to positively discriminate in their favour in any way that we can. The establishment of black literature collections, is a definite contribution librarians could make *now*. Needless to say, this has been done successfully for many years in major libraries in the United States, where every branch library has a clearly marked and well-used 'Black Studies' collection. Whatever one might think about race relations there, at least sophisticated people have long got beyond using the argument that to establish such collections is unnecessarily divisive! In New York Public Library is the magnificent Schomberg Collection, built up over the years to be the biggest library of books by and about black people in the world. How wonderful it would be if a large public library in this country were to recognize the incalculable value of establishing such a reference collection in England! Wonderful, but extremely unlikely.

Many libraries in the United States too, have become actively involved in literacy projects in their local communities. Surely this makes sense. Illiteracy is a problem affecting both adults and children. The library is in an ideal situation at least to co-operate in providing suitable materials for those trying to cope with illiteracy. How can illiteracy fail to be a matter of concern to librarians?

# 6
# Attitudes to Children's Books

It is obvious that there should be interchange of bookstock, and interchange of librarians working with adults and children. However, there will always need to be librarians who, although superficially aware of the potential of the entire bookstock, will concentrate on one aspect of it. Librarians working mainly with children will need time to build up a knowledge of the bookstock. They will need time to observe the gaps, and to test the stock against the children using it. An individual stock fluctuates constantly, and needs constant attention. As I said earlier, children keep being born. By giving continuous and intelligent attention to stock, staff will build up a picture which is less fallible than just using the number of times a book has issued as a guide. Also, they will be meeting and talking to children continually. This is where librarians have the advantage over other people involved in the children's book world—that is, writers, artists, publishers and reviewers. Librarians are constantly meeting endless varieties of children. That is not to say that other people do not have any contact with children. Many of them do, and naturally many have children of their own. But, excluding those writers who are also teachers, there is not likely to be one of them who comes into contact with such a wide cross-section of children as the most green children's librarian. This should be where our greatest strengths lie as librarians, in this matter of books. We should read widely and critically. We should use our professional training and our considered judgement in assessing books. But we should never forget children. They are, after all, what it is all about. It would plainly be ridiculous to suggest that books should only be written to suit the requirements of children. That is nonsensical. I would not deny that writers whose books have only a minority appeal should be published. I would, however, suggest that if a writer is hardly read by children, this factor should be recognised and taken into account when assessing the contribution of that writer to children's books. The truth is that it is frequently ignored by people who do not work with children, and so can conveniently forget about them. Librarians should never fall into this trap. They should know that a children's book which is enjoyed almost exclusively by adults cannot be acclaimed as a successful book for children, whatever its literary merits. If we review books we never need to resort to the ploys still occasionally used by reviewers of children's books in fashionable periodicals doing their obligatory Christmas books number, who make such comments as 'My eight-year-old son thought this book the most exciting of the batch', as though one individual child's opinion could be considered valid in this context. Would a reviewer of adult books ever expect to get away with a remark like 'My brother enjoyed this book'? It would be considered totally unprofessional. There are too many people who dabble in children's books and are given the opportunity to express their views in public. Two years ago a trendy Sunday newspaper, giving support to a children's book exhibition, decided to splash a feature on one new book selected from recent publications. This same book had been generally recognised in the children's book world as a piece of gimmicky publishing aimed at adults, which it was a shame to inflict on children. An individual children's book rarely gets such publicity. Why, when it happens, should be it given to a bad book, which has since sunk without trace, rather than to a real book? Librarians should be vociferous about this kind of thing, because librarians should know children and books. I believe that librarians should also stamp hard on attempts to generalise about books in a facile way. Naturally the pressures to prescribe specific books for specific age groups are great, but surely any experienced librarian should resist them except in the most general terms? Whenever I receive (and I do, too often) one of those letters from a College of Education student doing 'research' into children's reading habits, which poses questions of a painfully naïve variety, such as 'What do ten-year-old boys read'? I always write back that the only answer I am prepared to give is in the form of another question 'What do forty-year-old men read'? The two questions are equally absurd. Children are people. Their infinite variety is something for which to be thankful. Librarians are often asked questions about the popularity of specific books, individual authors or categories of books, and I think we should always resist the temptation to comment except in broad terms hedged about with qualifications. The practising children's librarian with some experience, who is meeting children day to day does have an instinct for this kind of thing, but it can never be more than that. Librarians with experience of more than one service point soon discover that it is not so easy to generalize, even at the superficial level of which books issue most frequently, as the answer from two libraries, even if they are less than half a mile apart, may well be different. I would not deny that there is a most fruitful field for intelligent research into many aspects of children's reading tastes and habits, but until that is done, comments on the subject should be suitably circumspect.

Librarians should be aware of all the opportunities there are for misunderstanding what books are for, and misusing them. If our starting point is that books should be for enjoyment, many such attitudes can easily be dismissed. Children's literature has always been a prey to the didacticism of adults, and always will be so. It is amusing to read about the redoubtable Mrs. Trimmer, who in 1802 founded a magazine, *The Guardian of Education*, the main object of which was to 'contribute to the preservation of the young and innocent from the dangers which threaten them in the form of infantine and juvenile literature'. Inspired by this noble ideal, one of her contributors wrote of *Cinderella* that it was:

Perhaps one of the most exceptionable books that was ever written for children. . . . It paints some of the worst passions that can enter into the human breast, and of which little children should, if possible, be totally ignorant; such as envy, jealousy, a dislike to mothers-in-law and half-sisters, vanity, a love of dress etc., etc.

We can laugh indulgently, but are we much better? Many statements made today about children's books will seem equally funny in fifty years time.

Probably in retrospect the worst failing of our age will be seen to be the tendency to want to *use* books—to prescribe them as a panacea for certain situations—the mania of bibliotherapy. So many people seem to want to fit books to specific situations of life in order to make them do something crudely and directly for the child who reads them. This is not the place to rehash banalities about the cathartic effects of the great tragedies of literature and so on—however, like so many distortions, the urge directly to use literature is a case of stretching a truism to absurdity, and a crude pinpointing of cause and effect which becomes utterly ludicrous. It shows a complete lack of any real appreciation of the essence of literature. A good example of what I mean can be seen in a booklet called *Situation Books for the Under-Sixes* by Hazel Bell. The blurb claims 'Whatever situation you and your child find yourselves in, Mrs. Bell has a book to suggest to match it'. So, under the heading *Eye-Patches and Glasses* we find the story of the rollicking pirate, *Captain Pugwash*, who wears a black eye-patch; under *Washing and Dressing Routines* is *Harry, the Dirty Dog*, in which Harry is only converted to taking baths after he spends a truant day playing by the railway, and sliding down a coal shute until he returns home so dirty that no one in the family recognizes him. Under *Death* comes Dick Bruna's version of Snow-White. The annotation is worth quoting:

> Snow-White is shown ensconced in her glass coffin, which might help children encountering a funeral; but the awkward question of resurrection arises as she wakes, young and beautiful as ever, when the poisoned apple is jerked from her throat.

Really! Of course young children respond to recognizable situations in books, often at a subconscious level, which explains the fierce devotion with which so many of them cling to a book like *Where the Wild Things are*, in which years ago Maurice Sendak caused consternation amongst some adults for daring to tackle the deep-rooted fears of young children in one of the most outstanding picture books of our time. At a simpler level I knew a small boy with poor eyesight, who first had to wear glasses at the age of three. For a time he could not be parted from *Borka, the Goose with no Feathers* by John Burningham, because one of the illustrations showed Borka's goose doctor, and he wore glasses. This was as it should be, an accidental discovery he made, and his own very individual response to a book.

Even the youngest children respond to books as individuals, and their response is related to their own experience.

There is no doubt that much interest in children's books has been generated in the past ten years by the development of organizations like the Pre-School Playgroup Association and the Federation of Children's Book Groups, which have helped to link together mothers concerned about their children's reading. Almost inevitably, I suppose, this has generated a great deal of earnestness too. Worries about the psychological implications of children's books are rampant, yet another example of our destructively self-conscious age. Giving talks to groups of young mothers, I find that they are always more concerned about the possible psychological effect of specific books or categories of books, notably traditional folk-tales, than they ever are about the possible effect of a steady diet of badly-written and sentimental books. From Mrs. Trimmer onwards, every generation of adults attacks folk-tales for different reasons. People curtail and bowdlerise them themselves if they cannot find suitably bowdlerized versions (like the mother I met recently who had Red Riding Hood marrying the woodcutter). The wisest and most humane, as well as the wittiest debunking of these tendencies is given in the chapter *The Battle for the Fairy Tale* in Kornei Chukovsky's *From Two to Five*, which should be compulsory reading for anyone interested in children and books. A critic had complained that one of Chukovsky's fantasy stories was harmful because it encouraged in children sympathy for a mosquito and other parasites; this was misleading, as on the one hand a ceaseless battle was being waged against insects throughout the country, and on the other a writer was leading children to feel sorry for them. Chukovsky pokes gentle fun at such attitudes, and at those people who seem to believe that a child soaks up and retains in the same form every fantasy absorbed in early childhood. As he points out:

Because a three-year-old child goes through a period when he likes to break toys, it does not follow that by the time he is fifteen he will have become a specialist in cracking fireproof safes.

A sense of humour, it is superfluous to say, is a sense of proportion. Unfortunately this characteristic is lacking in too many people involved in children's books. Highbrow reviewers make pretentious claims for books; less sophisticated reviewers become entangled in irrelevant side-issues which are nothing to do with what it *should* be all about. A conference of what sounded like fairly senior librarians in 1971 issued a series of inane comments on several books they had discussed, at the same time sending out a clarion call for 'a perceptive psycho-sociological survey of children's reading habits'. What *did* they mean? One of my favourite anecdotes is about a meeting of the Child Study Association of America, which I attended in New York in 1963. The children's book committee was meeting to discuss a short list of titles to go on a forthcoming list of recommended books. They were a formidable and intelligent group of women. However, the discussion foundered when they came to *Shadow of a Bull* by Maia Wojciechowska (Rodman). This was the story of the son of a famous bullfighter, expected by everyone to follow in his dead father's footsteps. The young man had no inclination to do so, and was haunted by the fear that he was a coward. Even so, he undertook the appropriate training, survived his first fight with honour, and announced that he would become a doctor. Everyone agreed that here was an enjoyable, compelling and well-written story. Then someone asked 'But do we really want to encourage an interest in bullfighting?' The arguments raged fiercely for twenty minutes, at which time the chairman ruled that everyone was becoming too heated, and the book would be referred for discussion at the next meeting! This same book later won the Newbery Medal.

I believe that this kind of attitude is laughable. I believe that crudely prescribing books like pills for specific situations is laughable. As always, analogies with adult literature point up the absurdity. Would anyone suggest that the relatives of an epileptic should read *The Idiot*, or that a person uncertain of his origins should read *Oliver Twist*?

However, it is valid to assess children's books critically with intelligence and perception, and to consider them within the framework of society. No one would claim this is always easy to do. It is possible not only to assess children's books as a whole, but also to assess them in relation to their readership, although this must be done with great care, and the pitfalls are many. It is for this reason that a group of London librarians, concerned that contemporary children's books failed to reflect our multi-racial society, undertook the compilation of a critically annotated survey of all children's books at that time in print on selected countries, *Books for Children: the Homelands of Immigrants in Britain*. We were all most concerned that this should be done in a thorough and systematic way, and that our assessment of each book should attempt to take all relevant factors into account. Nothing in our view was more dangerous than to isolate a single factor and base our judgement on that alone. Hence it was necessary to look at all the books on a specific country and evaluate them in relation to one another. Obviously, two of our main concerns were that there are children's books which reveal shockingly biased and prejudiced attitudes towards black people; also that children whose families had settled here, could find little on Cyprus or the West Indies which gave an authentic account of the country from which they or their parents had come to England. The first logical step was to survey the available material, and criticize it to the best of our ability. We felt that we must do more than produce a list of recommended books; it was important to include those we thought mediocre or totally unacceptable. One of the chief points of disagreement we had with our national YLG Committee, when we asked if they would publish the survey, was that they felt it would be better if our approach was less *negative*, and we omitted the bad titles. To us, this seemed a chronic failure to understand our purpose. We thought it was a small *positive* contribution we could make—an expression of our sense of social responsibility—to point out the prejudiced books within the framework of a complete survey.

Anyone who reads must be aware of the problem of identity which faces the black child growing up in our society; of the deep roots of prejudice, and our slow awareness of this—too slow to save that child from hurt, rejection and bitterness. To begin to understand we must read, and Fanon's *Black Skin, White Masks* is an essential starting point. If any librarian who works with children has not yet read Chris Searle's *The Forsaken Lover*, then this should be remedied at once. For here, in a book based on his experience teaching English in Tobago, is a sensitive and moving account of the problems of identity experienced by the black child being educated in a cultural tradition which denies his identity in the very language he has to use. Professional literature from the United States is full of discussions about racial prejudice and books, and has been for many years. I think such discussions are extremely important, and there should be more of them in *our* professional periodicals. (Or should I say *some* rather than more—so far they are generally conspicuous by their absence.)

However, unless they are based on two things, a real and deep understanding of racism in Britain, and a wide and critical knowledge of books as well as a sophisticated awareness of issues of censorship and freedom, it will be impossible to be truly constructive, and may be damagingly unconstructive. No other issues can cause so much anguish and concern. I have always believed that criticism of children's books should be uncompromisingly blunt. Certainly books should be criticized with care and in context, otherwise we shall be seen to be as absurd and ripe for counter-attack as ever Mrs. Trimmer's correspondent about *Cinderella* was. For this reason, much as I sympathize with the aims of Teachers against Racism, I regretted that their response to a request for their opinion of *Little Black Sambo* was to organize a meeting and issue a hurried statement condemning it, which did not even put the book in its historical context, or take into account any of the articles written about it in the past ten years or so, since it became an obvious talking point, particularly in the United States. As it was, their statement was a gift to anyone experienced in critical discussion of literature, and was used as such by Brian Alderson who had great fun at their expense in an article in *The Times*. Predictably this gave rise to a spate of mainly racist letters on the subject. My own views on this book are stated in an article in *The Times Literary Supplement*. I am also in sympathy with the aims of the Inter-Racial Council on Children's Books in the United States, but find some of the articles in their news sheet quite ludicrous. One such recently analysed the young children's picture books of Ezra Jack Keats, a white American, whose books have a black hero, a small boy named Peter, who grows older as the books progress. Probably the best, and one of the earliest, *The Snowy Day*, which tells very simply the experiences of a child playing in the snow, never fails to engage the attention of the under-fives. Each book is scrutinized and related to contemporary history from the civil rights movement to the rise of Black Power in an attempt to denigrate Keats as a classic white liberal whose books reflect his own shifting attitudes in the light of political developments. I find this alarming as well as ludicrous.

Talking of children's books and society, there is another issue which always arouses much comment and heated argument. Despite frequent protestations to the contrary, the ambience of the majority of English children's books is still comfortably middle-class. It cannot escape the librarian working in the average English community that most children are not. Before pens are dipped in vitriol to produce the usual violent reactions, I must hasten to add that I am making a generalized statement, and am neither implying that all children's books should have a working class ambience, nor that working class children should only read books about people like themselves. Predictably, most of the people who write, illustrate, publish and review children's books come from a middle-class background, and so it would be surprising if their books were otherwise. This merely mirrors the structure of our society. It was always so. As Harvey Darton wrote in his introduction to Children's Books in England:

> And children's books, written as such, have been in England almost entirely a product of the large domesticated middle-class, which began to exist, free of civil war, not wildly excited about religion nor very heedful of political arts, but increasingly conscious and desirous of freedom, under the Hanoverian dynasty.

Naturally, whenever attention is drawn to this, people get furious, and all the stock responses are trotted out. If you talk about the child's need for identification in this context, someone is sure to ask whether you think children living in high rise flats *really* want to read about children living in high rise flats; or someone else will produce the example of a real child they knew from a chronically deprived family who adored reading books by the most élitist writer the speaker can think of; or someone else will indignantly enquire whether it is being suggested that writers should be encouraged to write novels about the problems of disadvantaged children?

Here is another situation which is wide open to misinterpretation.

Children, like adults, need all kinds of different books at different times and in different moods. But one thing is certain: the need to identify with familiar experience (which doesn't exclude the need to identify with unfamiliar experience). That is all. There is a great gulf between children's books and children for many reasons, but this is one of them. Class-consciousness is deep-rooted in English life, and this fact is naturally mirrored in children's books as it is in other aspects of life. Not always in the subject matter of novels, but often in the tone, and certainly in the cadences of reported speech. Many people of course would deny it, and that is why they get so indignant. The reaction to the publication of *Nippers* in 1967 was proof of this. This series of easy readers, deliberately concentrated on stories about everyday life written in a lively and down-to-earth way, aimed to counteract the legions of easy readers about families living in an environment and speaking a language totally alien to the urban flat-dwelling child. Leila Berg, the editor, who has also written some of the stories, has received floods of letters, very many of them enthusiastic, and very many of them highly indignant. The latter are the most interesting, and in *Look at Kids* she recounts some of the reactions:

Heads wrote in about these books, scandalized and vehement, from both middle-class and slum areas. Such subjects, they said, should not be mentioned. Such subjects did not exist. Children do not play on bomb-sites or dumps. There are no bomb-sites or dumps. They have all been built over long ago (this was the beginning of 1967). All children play in parks or pleasant play areas. All homes have hot and cold water and proper bathrooms, and nobody uses tin baths. Fish and chips must not be mentioned. No children play in old cars. The head of the family must not be held up to criticism.

It was evident that some heads flatly denied their pupils' identity. Also they had no sense of humour.'

Children's books cannot be isolated from the society of which they are part. There is no easy answer. Understandably statements about the lack of books relevant to any section of the community can easily evoke a facile response and a rush to produce tenth-rate books by people who happen, for example, to come from a working-class background or to be black, but are not necessarily writers. Nothing would be more disastrous than forcing the growth of a second-rate literature by those whose social conscience is stronger than their skill as writers. Carried to its logical conclusion, this attitude would result in writers generally being restricted to writing about what they have experienced first hand, which is obviously absurd. However, there is an urgent need for *writers*. It has always been dangerous to pinpoint gaps in children's books. Publishers are usually snowed under by inadequate manuscripts anyway. All of us in the book world are confronted continually by people who think it is easy to write children's books. One of the most amusing examples in my experience was when I gave one of my standard talks to a playgroup supervisor's course, and made forceful comments about the lack of good picture books for the under-fives, coupled with equally forceful comments about the importance of vital language in books for young children, and how much skill and experience were required to write even an adequate story. A few days later, I received a manuscript from the husband of one of the women on the course. He had been so impressed by what she had told him of my talk that he sat down after supper, fired with enthusiasm, and tossed off an excruciatingly dull and predictable little story, which he hoped would help to alleviate the situation.

Just as it was necessary to establish that children's librarianship was an important and specialist branch of librarianship, which then led to children's librarians becoming isolated, so it is with children's books. The reason that so many books for children are not good enough is that people do not take children's books seriously. But it is also true that many people now take them *too* seriously, in the wrong way, with equally disastrous results. Many of us are becoming increasingly worried by the *intensity* of those who want to *use* children's books—supremely by those who see literature as an educational tool, and seem anxious to extract from it some tangible and concrete use to parallel the usefulness of books which feed facts into the child. I heard of someone working with the under-fives in Lambeth recently who rightly enthused about that delightful picture book, *The Very Hungry Caterpillar* in which the hero literally eats his way through holes in the pages, emerging at the end as a dazzlingly beautiful butterfly. However, she said it was so good because it was *educational* and was a valuable lesson in natural history!

Equally alarming are those who seem to have taken up children's books with fearful intensity. I am not alone in having kept away from the series of conferences organized at Exeter in recent years. By all accounts, people go there for a whole week and even talk children's books at breakfast. There is nothing wrong in discussing children's books, but nowadays people seem to get the whole thing out of proportion. I find disturbing, too, the emphasis on writers at Exeter. I have very much enjoyed knowing a number of writers of children's books in the course of my professional career. It can be extremely valuable and stimulating to hear an articulate writer talk about writing. But this occasion seems to have degenerated into a kind of jamboree, with writers as stars, reading aloud from their work, but also subjected to the kind of inquisitive interest usually accorded by our society to television personalities, and also to impertinent suggestions from ill-informed people about what sort of books the author *should* write. I was invited to speak at a weekend conference recently, which turned out to be a kind of off-shoot of Exeter. Groups of adults spent seven and a half hours spread over the weekend with each group discussing *one* children's book throughout that time. The sessions culminated in a confrontation with the author (with the exception of the unfortunate group who had opted for *Treasure Island*—their author didn't show up). I heard someone suggest that it was *necessary* to meet authors to fully understand their books. This is sheer nonsense. Does anyone ever suggest that it would help to understand *Couples* or *Jerusalem the Golden* if you met John Updike or Margaret Drabble? It might, but equally it might not. An author reveals as much as is necessary in a book, and if it can't be appreciated without knowing the author, it's a poor book. Imagine the complications if we all had to rush around trying to meet authors of books we are anxious to understand! And isn't it a bit hard on those who are dead—we can never hope to completely know what they were on about! This is a good example of the distortions that happen when things get out of proportion. It was sad to find at this conference several teachers who had come in the hope that they were going to be able to discuss with others working with children and books how to get books across to children, which books in the experience of others at the conference children enjoyed, and similar very important matters.

The children's book world is a tiny world, which tends to be dominated by a small group of people. The same names recur with predictable frequency whenever any aspect of children's books is under discussion. Up to a point this is inevitable, in such a miniature field of specialisation. Almost inevitably too, the focal point tends to be London. There is ample scope for intelligent and articulate librarians to bring a breath of fresh air into the children's book world. Perhaps the most worrying thing is that many people in it seem to think it *is* the world!

What is the record of the YLG on books? Unfortunately it has had little impact in recent years. One of the most glaring examples of failure is seen in the annual Library Association Medal Awards. The dreariness of this annual non-event has been mentioned elsewhere. Perhaps more distressing is the choice of books. There have been some inspired choices and some excellent writers and illustrators have been recognized. However, that said, there are far too many books on the list of past winners, particularly of the Carnegie Medal, which any honest librarian should have recognized as dead ducks from the start. I know all the arguments about books which seemed good in their time, but have now dated. I know that it is important to maintain critical standards whatever is meant by such a blanket phrase, and I know some of the difficulties involved in making a choice. I was on the committee the year no Carnegie Medal winner was selected in 1967. What I find inexcusable is the bowing to the fashionable, the safe and the tasteful, and the complete disregard for the reactions of children apparent in so many of the choices. Naturally, children's reactions shouldn't be the dominating factor—if they were the award would continually have gone to names librarians prefer to sweep under the carpet. But shouldn't children's reactions at least be relevant and taken into account? Is it any wonder that people continue to write books children don't read if librarians appear sublimely indifferent to whether children read the books to which they give awards or not? Here too may be part of the answer to the point made earlier about the boringly tasteful and staid appearance of so many books. One clause in the terms of the Carnegie Award reads: 'Format should be taken into account'. Looking at rows of medal winners, one is forced to the inevitable conclusion that librarians of all people are impressed by tastefully produced books. *Librarians* choosing books children don't read in formats they don't like? I am afraid that is just what they have done too often. Aidan Chambers has written very succinctly and forthrightly about this in Chapter 4 of *The Reluctant Reader*. It is mortifying that the selectors of the children's annual fiction award instituted by *The Guardian* have almost consistently shown more acumen in choice of book, and certainly more sophistication in the analysis of the reasons for their choice, than YLG. In fact, the latter have never yet been able to produce a properly reasoned explanation for some of the totally inexplicable choices which have been made. There was much public discussion of the Award, mainly in the columns of *The Times Literary Supplement* in 1968. Much argument led to little change. Like many librarians I know, and certainly most of the younger generation, I tend to ignore the medals, but I thought it worth mentioning because there are people, including children's librarians abroad, who take them seriously. It is very sad that the only official recognition we give to the work of authors, artists and publishers is such a damp squib. Needless to say, the Medals have no impact at all on the world outside children's books. There have been many instances when the Awards have been announced, and given to books which we did not even stock in Lambeth. On no such occasion do I recall that the pressure of popular demand, or even the interest of one reader, caused us to buy a copy of the titles in question.

YLG has an equally unfortunate record as far as the publication of booklists is concerned. In 1968 came a long-heralded booklist: *First Choice*, subtitled *A Basic Booklist for Children* and consisting of 665 titles, the aim of which as stated in the preface was 'to produce a list of books of high quality which could be recommended as the basic stock of any children's library'. The list was not impressive. It showed no evidence of the previously mentioned unique contribution that the librarian can bring to criticism—an awareness of real, live children and their response to books. It included a great deal of dead wood, and showed a curious lack of flair for the books which were both good and popular with children at that time. Subsequent general booklists have been unsatisfactory too. Since 1969 an annual list has been published, in each case of one hundred assorted books, not confined to new publications, to any specific age range or any specific subject. The thinking behind these lists is muddled, so it is hardly surprising they have little impact. Why a hundred books? What criteria were used for selection? Why were the first two lists the work of one person, when the Publications Committee could have drawn on the entire membership? The annotations, frequently sloppily written and rarely more than one sentence in length, beg more questions than they answer. YLG is a national professional organization. The general lists they produce lack the authority they should have. This has always been true. More substantial lists published in the past, such as *Books for Young People*, were similarly uninspired, and I found them no use at all in my early days as a practising children's librarian. Is it too much to hope that librarians will ever be bibliographically adventurous and imaginative? Will they ever produce lists that are not utterly predictable? I would not deny that the special lists have been better. *Stories to Tell* was of a much higher standard, and was extremely useful, as is the recent *Books for the Multi-Racial Classroom* although marred by the distressing but obviously unconscious insensitivity of listing novels which included black children among the characters under the general heading *Problems*. The fact remains that librarians through their national organization do not seem able to publish general lists as useful as those compiled by other people. To give two reasonably current examples: The *Reading for Enjoyment* lists edited by Nancy Chambers, have distinct individuality and credibility. There is an air of professionalism and authority about them which YLG lists consistently lack. The annotations are intelligent, and long enough to be both descriptive and critical. It is sad but true that few librarians show evidence of being able to write annotations anyway. Since 1970, *Children's Books of the Year* selected and annotated by former librarian and well-known reviewer Elaine Moss, has proved a refreshing and informed guide to recent books. Essentially the choice is personal, and all the better for it when the selection is made by someone with as much experience, and grasp of essentials as Elaine Moss. Her own enthusiasm is communicated through her very readable annotations. Her lists have a sense of confidence and sure judgement—characteristics the YLG lists conspicuously lack. I am quite sure there must be many practising children's librarians throughout the country who, working as a team could produce viable lists. Perhaps it is just that YLG never takes the trouble or hasn't the mechanics to seek them out?

Certainly, children's librarians do read children's books. I have met people who even read children's books for their own personal enjoyment; just as I have known some who read *only* children's books. My own view, stated elsewhere, is that a continual diet of children's books is bound to lead to gradual softening of the brain. I have always considered reading children's books as an exercise carried out on behalf of children, and that it would be very odd if I reacted to them as profoundly and with the same pleasure as I do to reading adult books.

We should never lose a sense of proportion about children's books, and should fight for them to be recognized and taken seriously, if not too seriously. We should be swift to condemn those who suggest it is easy to write for children, and that any idiot could do it. Attitudes to children's books are probably similar throughout the world. As Arviette, the budding writer in *Cancer Ward* says:

. . . Gorky said 'Anyone can become a writer'. With hard work anyone can achieve anything. If the worst comes to the worst I can become a children's writer. Anyone can do that.

On the other hand, we should not become so enchanted and limited by involvement in children's books that we forget that they should be essentially a passing phase, and that children should be encouraged to move on from them as soon as they are ready. This fact was noted many years ago in the days when children's books were considerably less plentiful than they are today, in a wise article by Charlotte M. Yonge, recently reprinted in *Signal*, which should prove a fitting end to this chapter:

After all, our conclusions as to children's literature is a somewhat Irish one, for it is—use it as little as possible. . . .

# Final Thoughts:
# A Personal Summing-up

There are many subjects I have not touched on. One is bookshops. In Lambeth, one of the largest inner boroughs of the capital city of England, what happens if a parent or a child has the urge to buy a children's book? There is a branch of W. H. Smith which stocks some of the adult titles which are being currently talked about and reviewed, and almost invariably none of the children's books in the same category, although they have a miserly selection of long-standing favourites, usually in the cheapest hardback editions, plus what can only be described as a quixotically random selection of paperbacks. At the time of writing, there is a tiny newly-established bookshop which hopes to extend to including some children's books; and a shop specializing in secondhand titles which has some children's books from a very limited range of publishers. Three department stores recognize what they call a 'seasonal demand' for children's books, and paperbacks appear before Christmas and disappear afterwards. There are almost as many children's books on sale in Woolworth's as anywhere else. Small stands in newsagent's shops carry a few of the most predictable paperbacks almost invariably by the most predictably popular writer. Anyone with the time who wants to buy a children's book can travel to small bookshops in outlying boroughs; or pay probably twice the price of an average children's paperback to journey into central London and back. Even there, whether anyone with a specific title in mind will find what they want is doubtful. I would never under-estimate the value of the Puffin Club for those who have joined it; or of the various bookselling schemes operated through schools and other agencies. The fact remains that it is not *easy* for a child in Lambeth to buy a real book.

Children need to own books. Libraries should encourage this in every way. We are only doing half our job by persuading children

to *borrow* books; we must also encourage them to *own* books for themselves. There should be books *everywhere* for people to borrow and
to buy. I recognize all the familiar arguments about the reasons for
this state of affairs. I know it is simplistic to suggest there should be
children's paperbacks on sale in supermarkets and launderettes. But
if this could be done, there might well be a *real* paperback revolution. People want to buy books, and will do so if it is as easy as
buying cigarettes. As things are, buying books requires a degree of
tenacity. I cannot count the number of times I have tried to buy a
specific and well-known children's book in London. It can take
visits to about five places before a copy is produced—and I know
my way around, as well as where to look first. It is tempting to wonder
whether the book trade has a death wish. Admittedly there are a few
superb bookshops in different parts of the country, but the overall
coverage is appalling. To find a knowledgeable assistant is rare. I
have frequently stood around in well-known London bookshops and
listened despairingly to the mis-information about children's books
being fed to customers.

Naturally, I think there should be bookshops in libraries, even if
they are independently run. But this would only be a solution to a
tiny part of the problem, because many people who might buy books
don't go near libraries. Every time we give informal talks to small
groups of young mothers, they are invariably interested in buying
paperback picture books provided they can do this with the same
ease they buy groceries—and why shouldn't they be able to?

I have made only fleeting references to young adults. This is
deliberate. Much as I believe we should pay more attention to the
reading needs of this age group, I regret that in Britain work with
young adults is always considered as an appendage to work with
children. I believe this is wrong, and that it should always be considered within the context of adult book provision, although there
will obviously be close links with children's books too. In Lambeth,
having failed to pay specific attention to the over-twelves in the past,
we are now just beginning to remedy this in a small way. This has
hardly been a failure unique to Lambeth, but on a national scale, not
redeemed by the fact that a few urban library systems have made
attempts to do something for this group and have been hailed as

pioneers for such allegedly revolutionary activities as providing coffee and pop music in libraries. County libraries have a much better record in this respect, but as I remarked earlier, many British librarians appear to live in a vacuum, totally oblivious to developments in the rest of the world. The vast body of literature about work with young adults in the United States alone is largely ignored here, and whenever the topic is raised, people can be heard re-hashing old arguments without any apparent awareness that the ideas they are suggesting have been discussed, tried, and fully documented elsewhere. As must be obvious in the light of our views about children we do not believe in separate libraries for teenagers in Lambeth. For this reason it was disappointing as well as misleading to find the young adult area of our West Norwood Library which opened in 1969 cited as an example of a specific 'teenage library' in *British Librarianship and Information Science 1966–1970*. That is what it most certainly is not. When this comprehensive library was planned (and it was well and truly planned at weekly meetings between architects and senior librarians over a long period) the aim was to recognize that certain groups in the community have particular needs at certain times which should be recognized in such a multi-purpose building as this. The young adult area (which like the rest of the library is not labelled in any way) was intended as a place for young people to relax and chat with friends, against a background of changing displays, including books. It would have been logical also to have had a geriatric browsing room. It had been intended to appoint a librarian based at West Norwood to work with young adults when the library opened, but financial cuts prevented this. This is one reason the area has never worked as well as it was hoped, except recently on occasions when folk groups and poetry reading sessions have taken place there.

I make no apology for having concentrated on ideas for taking the library services out to those who use them least and possibly need them most, because I believe that is where out greatest challenge lies. It matters that we should always strive to provide a good service for those people who do use libraries, and I would never underestimate the importance of this. However, I still think more of our energies in future should be directed to those who do not use them.

I also make no apology for writing about library work with children in an urban context. More has tended to be written on the subject in relation to county libraries in recent years, particularly in relation to services to schools. County library systems seem generally to be showing more enterprise and ideas than municipal libraries. In parts of England library services to children have only reached a rudimentary level. It would no doubt surprise people outside the children's book world to know that included in this category are three of the largest cities in England, namely Manchester, Liverpool and Leeds. I recognize the irony in suggesting that children's library services should become fully integrated into services to all people, when some of them barely exist.

I have confined my comments and illustrations to areas within my own personal experience in Lambeth and in New York Public Library. If I had chosen to survey the whole field, and everything that is being done by other people in each of these areas, I should have written a different kind of book. My aim has been to show, mainly to new entrants to the profession and to interested outsiders, what is being done in one library system. I have done this deliberately to counteract other books about library work with children published in this country which are so generalized as to be little help to those who want to know what it is actually *like* to work with children in a public library.

Because I am an enthusiast, and unquenchably optimistic about the possibilities of everything we do, I recognize that some people might think that everything we do in Lambeth is successful, that nothing ever goes wrong, and that I am suggesting everyone should try the same pattern. Nothing could be further from the truth. I have tried to use my experience in Lambeth to show that there is nothing spectacular about the things we do. Everything is developing logically from thinking continually about the changing role of libraries in society, and how this should apply in a specific area of London. We are all learning to work and plan together, not just within the library service, but within the entire Directorate. It would be unreal to imagine that everything *works*. Because we are always in a state of flux and change all of us are constantly being made aware of the weaknesses in our system. We also constantly make mistakes.

We still think this is better than to maintain a calm level of efficiency, and never to experiment. Staff in Lambeth are encouraged to be critical, and no one could be more critical of our services than we are. I hope as time goes on that we shall reach more sophisticated levels of researching and evaluating the things we do, although I believe that our 'success' is something it is not possible to measure, as there is no way of doing this satisfactorily.

I may be optimistic, but I am also a realist. If it is part of our brief to try and reach every one of the child population in the borough with books, nothing is more certain than that we have hardly begun to grapple with this yet. Take the summer storytelling programme. It sounds good to say that a team of twenty-seven storytellers visited forty-six sites each week during the holidays. But just recall some of the housing estates described earlier. How much help to these children is one storytelling session a week lasting for twenty-five minutes? I believe it is better than nothing, but it is an infinitesimal contribution seen in perspective. The same is true of everything we do. There are thousands of deprived children we never reach in any way at all. How many of those we do reach can read fluently enough to enjoy it, or ever find a book which means anything to them?

I do believe that libraries must develop and change as the world around us is changing. Without this we can have no hope of survival, and no chance of making the *real* contribution we could make to the communities we serve. Large scale local government is almost here. New and larger authorities will be created. There will be opportunities for new thinking, and new changes of direction. Will we seize them?

I have been harsh about librarians. It is because so much *should* be asked of all of us. Librarianship is potentially a most absorbing and exciting profession which demands *real* commitment from those of us who try to practice it. It is difficult not to be impatient with those who are content to continue working in well-worn grooves, conscientious, but anxious to avoid conflict, change, and anything which would disturb the even tenor of their professional lives.

There is so much to do in librarianship. There is a great need for people with vision, energy, drive and imagination. Above all, there is a need for people with a sense of *urgency*. Sir Alec Clegg concluded his lecture *Recipe for Failure*, quoted earlier, with a sentence intended to shock his listeners into realising that action must be taken immediately to help those children whose educational development is irretrievably limited by their social conditions. He could have been speaking to those of us who also work with children, as librarians:

There is still time for us to learn, but it is getting short.

# Appendix I

## ELEANOR FARJEON ACCEPTANCE SPEECH*

May I say first that the microphone and rather battered equipment I am using I brought here for sentimental reasons, as it is the equipment we use for our out-door storytelling programme in Lambeth. Of course, this is a very different gathering. You need not worry: I shall not tell you a story. The audience, too, is quite different. I am reasonably confident that none of you will rush up to pull out the appropriate plug and so reduce me to utter silence; nor that, as I finish, anyone will seize the microphone in the hope of shouting a rude word down it before I switch off.

I feel very honoured to be standing here tonight as the winner of the Eleanor Farjeon Award—not just because of the award, but because of the setting and the beauty of this hall and the gracious occasion which the Children's Book Circle always provides. I've been to Eleanor Farjeon receptions before, but till now hadn't realized anything of the hard work that goes on behind the scenes. I should particularly like to thank Paul Langridge and Joanna Goldsworthy for all that they have done for this ceremony. It is always the most civilized event of the children's book world year—there is no question about that—and I know we all appreciate it very much.

This is an especially moving occasion for me, because I am the first librarian to win the Award; also, because I see here so many people who in their different ways contribute so much to the children's book world. If I named them all, you would be here all night, so I'll just say what particular pleasure it gives me to see Grace Hogarth Sayles and her husband here tonight: like many other people involved in children's books in England, I owe a great deal to Grace.

More than any previous recipient of this award, I think, I am a representative

*An edited, slightly expanded version of the talk given by Miss Hill at the Eleanor Farjeon Award celebration on 25 May, 1972, at Carpenters Hall, London. The award, made by the Children's Book Circle, is given annually for distinguished services to children's books during the preceding year. Janet Hill received the award in particular recognition of her editorship of *Books for Children*: *The Homelands of Immigrants in Britain*, published by the Institute of Race Relations. Reprinted from *Signal*.

of many groups of people. No library service develops in isolation, and an effective library service needs first of all the encouragement, as well as the financial support, of an interested Council; that is why I am very pleased that Councillor Rigger, Chairman of Lambeth's Amenities Committee, is here tonight.

No children's librarian works in isolation, either: our achievements in Lambeth happen because of the scope given by Roy McColvin, our Director, to his staff. I've worked with him for fifteen years, and have found this a continuing challenge. I'm sure he won't mind if I call him a man with a restless mind. He is constantly querying everything that one does, and making one improve on it. I think my favourite memory of him is from the days when he was Deputy Librarian. We would tour round all the branches on the first day of Children's Book Festival to look at the exhibitions; I would start to be elated—or depressed —and he'd say, 'Now Janet, this year's Festival is as good as over. I really think that next year we should aim to. . . .'

I'm glad, too, that our Assistant Director, Ted Rubidge, is here; his infinite tact and understanding are a tremendous source of strength to all the staff in Lambeth. And then there's Jenny Evans, my assistant. I get ideas, but I'm not the world's most practical person, as Jenny could tell you nightmare stories to prove. But Jenny has that unusual combination of imaginativeness and practicality, and without her a lot of the things that happen in Lambeth couldn't happen at all. She and I are supported by an enthusiastic and dedicated staff represented here by Margaret Brice and John Stunell.

Nothing could have pleased me more than to receive the Eleanor Farjeon Award specifically for editing *Books for Children*: it was an exercise that symbolized what I believe a librarian should try to do—always to have one foot in books and one foot in the world. (Here again, the work on this survey was done by fourteen librarians, working extremely hard over a three-year period, and it is good that they are well represented here today—also that we have with us Simon Abbott, Assistant Director of the happily reprieved Institute of Race Relations. Without his co-operation and the editorial work of his staff in the final stages, the list would never have seen the light of day.) I can't pretend we didn't have colleagues who advised us that it would be much more tactful to produce a list simply of recommended titles. But we were determined that this was not the way to do it.

I firmly believe that librarians should say what they think about books, but without arrogance. Anyone who works with books essentially has a feeling of humility about the work done by writers, artists and editors, and all those who contribute to making a book. However, the librarian has a unique contribution to make too, because the librarian is in contact with children. I must admit that it is sometimes hard not to feel a bit superior when reviewers or publishers quote reactions of a rather small sample of children to books, particularly when the children are usually relatives or the children of friends. Naturally, those of us who are supervising rather than practising librarians no longer have the right to claim we know with such certainty what children are reading, but we can draw on the varied experience of our staff who are still in touch daily with great numbers of children. The knowledge we have should be used with intelligence. There will always be the temptation to indulge in superficial generalizations, because it is hard for anyone else to prove us wrong, and because there will be every encouragement from the mass media, or from students on projects, to produce lists of the most popular writers, or the kind of books most read by eleven-year-old girls, and other meaningless exercises which overlook many factors, supremely the individuality of reading tastes. However, this knowledge can be used constructively to point out the books to which children do *not* respond, and the truth is that they are often the ones highly praised by adults. It is because librarians see books in relation to children that our views should be forcefully expressed, and that we should take every opportunity to express them. If there are books which are not good enough for children, for whatever reason, librarians should be the first to say so. And so I am more than pleased that, having made some extremely caustic comments about books in the survey, I have been given an award for it.

Of course, it can be a dangerous practice, this business of categorizing books, of looking for certain things in books. That is why I feel that our approach— undertaking a large-scale survey of books on a number of countries—was essential. In considering isolated books, looking at them only for certain factors, we could have got a totally unbalanced view. I rather enjoyed reading an extract from a paper given at a conference on sexism in children's books in the United States. I quote: 'Cop-out books are those which start out right, but compromise somewhere, such as the tomboy who becomes a lady etc. Even such an excellent character as Kit in *Witch of Blackbird Pond* has as her main worry who "he" will be.' For those of you who know *Witch of Blackbird Pond*, an enjoyable and readable historical novel set in seventeenth-century Connecticut—what a ludicrous comment! What could an enterprising girl do at that time and in that place except look for her man!

No, if one is going to criticize, that criticism must be justified; otherwise, it merely develops into a witch hunt against individual books. I know that I tend to go on rather about mediocre books, and I do want to pay tribute to the wonderful books that are produced: to the writers and artists, many of whom I have the pleasure of knowing; and the editors, many of whom, I work with. But I think librarians feel so strongly about the mediocrity in books because they are constantly in touch with children. I know from working in Lambeth, where there are a lot of children who are not likely to come into natural contact with books, that unless this happens through their schools, libraries, or other agencies, it could be possible for a child never to have read a book that was anything but mediocre—a terrifying thought. I believe that reading is for enjoyment, and should be for enjoyment; the only way that children will come to read is if they have actually found books which give them a feeling of enjoyment. Every book should be an experience. Perhaps this is a tall order, but I believe it to be true.

Reading is assailed on many sides, and comments are always being made about reading and television, reading and other interests, and so on. I'm sure people don't read as much now as they did even twenty years ago. There are exceptions to this, and whenever there is talk about people depending on books I am always reminded of George Jackson and his very moving letters in *Soledad Brother*, revealing how he educated himself in prison between the ages of eighteen and twenty-nine and what books meant to him during his short and tragic life, because he wasn't exposed to all the distractions we claim take people from books. He wrote about his earliest experience of confinement in the Chino Reception Centre:

In my early prison years I read all of Rafael Sabatini, particularly *The Lion's Skin*. 'There was once a man who sold the lion's skin while the beast still lived and was killed while hunting him.' This story fascinated me. It made me smile even under the lash. The hunter bested, the hunted stalking the hunter. The most predatory animal on earth turning on its oppressor and killing it. At the same time, this ideal existed in me just above the conscious level. It helped me to define myself, but it would take me several more years to isolate my real enemy. I read Jack London's 'raw and naked, wild and free' military novels and dreamed of smashing my enemies entirely, overwhelming, vanquishing, crushing them completely, sinking my fangs into the hunter's neck and never, never letting go.

Capture, imprisonment, is the closest to being dead that one is likely to experience in this life. There were no beatings (for me at least) in this youth joint and the food wasn't too bad. I came through it. When told to do something I simply played the idiot, and spent my time reading. The absentminded bookworm, I was in full revolt by the time seven months were up.

Throughout the letters there are references to books, and George Jackson wrote with increasing fluency and confidence as his political consciousness developed through reading and experience of prison life. Of course, no one would wish his situation on any other human being; but his life shows the power books can have.

What I think we should be trying to do as librarians is to give children the opportunity of meeting books wherever they are. I don't have illusions about creating whole generations of bookworms in Lambeth. Some children will read avidly, some will read only occasionally; but we must make sure that every child will somehow find books that mean something to him personally—whichever books do this—so that he can see reading as an enjoyable activity.

Under the dryer this morning, I was reading Leila Berg's new book, *Look at Kids*. She writes in a tremendously sensitive and heartfelt way of the dilemma of the urban child, over-crowded, often unwanted, brushed off by busy parents, and the difficulties such children have:

Once, when working with a group of children from problem families (the same group who preferred pretend tea to real tea), I tried to explain to a social worker of a supposedly non-authoritarian organization why I was writing the children's names on chairs, on hooks, on the wall, on table mats, on everything possible, in every colour of the rainbow; they were the only under-fives I have ever met who made no response to the sound of their own name: 'I'm trying to get them to know their own identity', I said. 'Oh, but is that a good idea,' she said, 'when each family only has one or two rooms to live in If the children have their own identity, it's going to cause a lot of trouble.'

Through reading, you can find some kind of individuality—and this is what I hope, what I'm sure, we are trying to do; to give children the chance of discovering their own identity.

It is heartening to feel that the most exciting developments in my job are yet to come. One of the most important things that happened in the creation of the new Directorate in Lambeth in 1970, when the library service became linked with the amenity services, was that the staff who run the sports centres and the pools, organize activities in parks, and all the other cultural and recreational activities in the borough, became part of the same set-up as the librarians. We are now all working together, and this has been an especially broadening experience for me: suddenly one realizes that we are all dealing with the same children; that all the services provided are important for the development of the whole child. Of course, we have hardly started yet. Although I have been a librarian for a long time, I feel now at the very beginning of everything that one could possibly do. Only now are we starting to get out into the community and meet children where they are.

All of you in your different ways contribute so much to making this possible, to making the books possible that we take into the community. I would like to say finally how much I value not only working with sports centre staff, but with publishers, booksellers, editors, meeting authors and artists, and everyone concerned in the making of books, and seeing how much your integrity contributes to the real and whole book.

# *Appendix II*

## BIBLIOGRAPHY

(*Author's note*: This is not a full professional bibliography as such. It is a source list of the books and periodicals which I have quoted in the preceding chapters.)

BALLINGER, John. *Children's reading halls*. Library Association Record, 5, 1903

BELL, Hazel. *Situation books for the under-sixes*. Kenneth Mason, 1970

BERG, Leila. *Look at kids*. Penguin, 1972

BOSTON, Lucy. *Memory in a House*. Bodley Head, 1973

CHAMBERS, Aidan. *The Reluctant Reader*. Pergamon, 1969

CHAMBERS, Nancy. (*Ed.*) *Reading For Enjoyment*. Four annotated lists available from The Children's Book Centre, 140 Church Street, London, W.8

CHAMBERS, Nancy. (*Ed.*) *Signal*. A journal published 3 times annually by The Thimble Press, Stroud, Glos.

CHUKOVSKY, Kornei. *From two to five*. (Translated by Miriam Morton). Rev. ed. University of California Press, 1968

CLEGG, Sir Alec. *Recipe for Failure*. National Children's Home Convocation Lecture, 1972

COARD, Bernard. *How the West Indian child is made educationally subnormal in the British school system*. New Beacon Books, 1971

COOK, Elizabeth. *The Ordinary and the Fabulous*. Cambridge University Press, 1969

DARTON, F. J. Harvey. *Children's books in England*. Cambridge University Press, 2nd ed. 1958

DAVIE, Ronald *and others*. *From birth to seven*. Longman/National Children's Bureau, 1972

DODSON, Dan. Address at American Library Association Conference Session, 1967

FANON, Frantz. *Black Skin, White Masks*. MacGibbon & Kee, 1968; Paladin, 1970

GEORGE, Jean. *My side of the mountain*. Bodley Head, 1962

HARROD, Roy. *Library work with children*. Deutsch, 1969

HILDICK, E. W. *Children and Fiction*. Evans, 1970

HILL, Janet. (*Ed.*) *Books for Children: The Homelands of Immigrants in Britain*. Institute of Race Relations, 1971

HILL, Janet. *Oh! Please Mr Tiger*. Times Literary Supplement, 3rd November 1972

ILLICH, Ivan. *Deschooling society*. Calder and Boyars, 1971

MCCOLVIN, Lionel R. *Libraries for children*. Phoenix, 1961

MILLER, Ruth. *Careers for girls*. Penguin, Rev. ed. 1970

MOSS, Elaine. *Children's Books of the Year*: 1970; 1971; 1972. Published annually by Hamish Hamilton in association with the National Book League

PEARCE, Philippa. *A dog so small*. Longman, 1962; Puffin, 1964

*Report of the Commisoner of Education's Committee on Library Development, University of State of New York*. The State Education Department, (Albany), 1970

SAYERS, Frances Clarke. *Anne Carroll Moore*. Hamish Hamilton, 1973

SAYERS, Frances Clarke. *Summoned by books*. Viking Press. 1965

SAYERS, W. C. Berwick. *Manual of children's libraries*. Allen and Unwin, 1932

SCHICKEL, Richard. *The Disney Version*. Simon & Schuster, 1968

SEARLE, Chris. *The Forsaken Lover*. Routledge & Kegan Paul, 1972; Penguin, 1973

SOLZHENITSYN, Alexander. *Cancer Ward*. Bodley Head, 1970; Penguin, 1971

YONGE, Charlotte M. *Children's literature of the last century*. First published Macmillan's magazine, 1869. Reprinted *Signal*, January 1971.

# Index